# Welfare States in the 21st Century

## The New Five Giants Confronting Societal Progress

Ian Greener

*Professor of Social Policy, University of Strathclyde, UK and Adjunct Professor, University of Adelaide, Australia*

Cheltenham, UK • Northampton, MA, USA

Published by
Edward Elgar Publishing Limited
The Lypiatts
15 Lansdown Road
Cheltenham
Glos GL50 2JA
UK

Edward Elgar Publishing, Inc.
William Pratt House
9 Dewey Court
Northampton
Massachusetts 01060
USA

Paperback edition 2023

A catalogue record for this book
is available from the British Library

Library of Congress Control Number: 2022931146

This book is available electronically in the **Elgar**online
Sociology, Social Policy and Education subject collection
http://dx.doi.org/10.4337/9781800370791

ISBN 978 1 80037 078 4 (cased)
ISBN 978 1 80037 079 1 (eBook)
ISBN 978 1 0353 2526 9 (paperback)

Printed and bound by CPI Group (UK) Ltd, Croydon, CR0 4YY

# Contents

# 1.   The Beveridge Report today

## INTRODUCTION

There are points in time where we have an opportunity to look back on where as a society we have come from, and think hard about where we should go next. In the UK, one such time is at an anniversary of the 1942 'Beveridge' Report (Beveridge 1942), which gave a compelling vision of five 'Giants' that needed to be overcome to achieve societal progress – Want, Disease, Ignorance, Squalor and Idleness. Although much of the 300-page report is taken up with the detail of proposals for changes to social security, it is the opening paragraphs, which include Beveridge's striking vision, that remain with us.

The year 2022 is the 80th anniversary of Beveridge's report, and the world has changed a great deal since the dark days of World War 2. There is an opportunity for renewal, especially in the wake of a global pandemic, for us to raise our heads from the everyday challenges we all face, and to think hard about where, together, we all want to go next. This book is an attempt to contribute to that debate.

This chapter, after the present introduction, outlines the original Beveridge Report in the context of its own time, before exploring what other writers have said in terms of the 'Giants' we might need to confront today. It then derives a list of criteria for being a 'New Giant'; these can be picked up in Chapter 2, where the choice of these New Giants is presented. Identifying possible New Giants is worthwhile in itself, as we will need all of our energies to deal with the big societal challenges we face. Chapter 2 outlines the 'New Giants' that will be explored in the book, giving reasons for their selection. However, the book also aims to go beyond identification, and to look to countries that are already having success in confronting these New Giants to see what we can learn from them.

Chapter 3 explains the book's method and data in detail, but it is worth giving a brief outline of that here as well. The book is comparative: if we are going to understand which countries appear to be making the most progress in dealing with the New Giants, we need to understand which countries are making the most progress in confronting them, what they might have in common, and how they are different.

The standard way of comparing and contrasting countries is linear model-ling. In that approach, models are constructed based on a range of factors that existing research suggests might be relevant in understanding what we are looking at. We then try to find equations that represent the data as best we can. However, this approach also comes with a range of problems, especially when dealing with country-level data.

First, there are only so many countries in the world; and within the group, there are even fewer that are reasonably comparable (it makes little sense to compare, for example, Canada and Liberia, as their history, infrastructure and politics are so different). Moreover, in very few instances are reliable data available for the countries (Babones 2013).

Second, linear models are useful where the countries for which we have data show variation across the range of values we are interested in, but this is seldom the case. Countries don't have every combination of factors – they tend to 'cluster' around particular patterns. There are only so many different ways democratic countries can configure their political systems. This problem is called 'limited diversity'. Third, linear models struggle when we are interested in how several different factors interact, but we have relatively few data items (the countries we are interested in).

A method designed to overcome these challenges, Qualitative Comparative Analysis (QCA), was developed by Charles Ragin (Ragin 2008, 2014) and has evolved significantly since its invention. It offers a means of rigorously comparing countries around a range of factors to see which appear to be achieving stronger performance against a set outcome, and then to see which factors appear to be important in that achievement. We will say more about this method in Chapter 3, but for the moment, please note that the book uses QCA for the reasons given above.

Chapters 4 to 8 take each of the book's 'New Giants', exploring them in relation to a range of causal factors, to try to understand not only which coun-tries appear to be making the most progress in relation to them, but also, using QCA, what they have in common.

The book presents its main conclusions in Chapter 9, identifying the coun-tries that appear to be making the most progress across all of the New Giants, and summarizing what we have learned from the separate chapters. Further to this, Chapter 10 considers the factors identified in Chapter 9 in relation to each country's response to COVID-19. This chapter was not a part of the original plan for the book, but felt like a necessary extension of it given the ongoing pandemic.

Before moving on to the New Giants though, the current chapter now turns to the original Giants identified by Beveridge, locating them in the context in which they arose, and outlining which 'New' Giants other authors have identified.

# THE BEVERIDGE REPORT IN CONTEXT

The Beveridge Report was published in 1942, just as World War 2 seemed to be turning towards the allied forces. At such a time, it was brave to even begin to consider what Britain would look like in the event of winning the war, and the visionary language contained within the report and the response to it from the British people meant that it became hugely important. On its anniversaries, writers concerned about the challenges the country is facing have an opportunity to wonder what a 'new' Beveridge Report might look like, in terms of which challenges it would identify, and what we might do to try to meet them.

The main focus of Beveridge's report was meant to be to consider what the expansion of existing social insurance systems and institutions might look like post-war. Beveridge achieved that remit, but in the language he used in its first paragraphs also presented a vision of what social policy post-war might look like. He famously identified the 'Five Giants' he regarded as blocking the path to civilized society as 'Want' (most similar to poverty in today's language), 'Disease' (which Beveridge said required the creation of a national health service), 'Ignorance' (which pointed to the creation of a free secondary school system), 'Idleness' (which was about how unemployed persons might be supported, and was an especially important topic given the inter-war economic depression) and 'Squalor' (which was concerned primarily with housing, but is probably best considered in terms of public health more generally).

Beveridge's report was primarily about addressing the Giant of 'Want', but also made reference to 'Idleness', as he was concerned with poverty amongst the unemployed. However, he also made clear that, if the government were to tackle Want and Idleness, it also had to extend social policy to deal with the other Giants he had identified. Specifically, he made three assumptions: that a national health service would be created to look after the nation's health; that families would be offered additional support through the creation of additional benefits linked to children; and that the government would seek to achieve full employment, which he defined as below 8.5% unemployment. If the latter does not sound radical, then in the context of the Great Depression of the previous decade, and at a time when, beyond the still-new work of Keynes (1997) represented a radical challenge to prevailing economic orthodoxies. At that time, the government was generally regarded as not having a role in dealing with unemployment, while Beveridge was putting forward a view of post-war economy and society that was very different to that of the 1930s.

Beveridge's plans, then, were ambitious. The wartime government was reluctant to adopt them, but a mix of public support (Beveridge was very good at publicizing his findings, and a summary of his report including the section on the Five Giants became a bestseller) and parliamentary pressure, especially from Labour members, meant that the government felt forced to consider it. Beveridge's plans were referred to various inter-war committees, eventually leading to recommendations that, although they adapted many of Beveridge's original recommendations, were certainly in the broader spirit of the changes he had proposed. A national health service was created, as were family allowances. The government took greater responsibility for dealing with unemployment than it had pre-war. An extended social security system was put in place, including both state pensions and improved access to benefits for the unemployed.

The visionary language of Beveridge's 'Giants' remains with us today, as does the idea that we might be able to step back from the day-to-day challenges we face, and look to see what big challenges our societies encounter. There are calls for a 'New Beveridge' to do that work (Coats 2020; Savage 2021) The next section explores what other writers and researchers have said in respect of this.

## NEW GIANTS IDENTIFIED IN EXISTING RESEARCH

A number of different researchers have presented their ideas on what updating Beveridge might represent.

In 1998, Anthony Giddens, a hugely important academic, but also a central figure in the development of progressive politics in the 1990s and 2000s (Giddens 1994), published perhaps his most influential book, *The Third Way* (Giddens 1998). Giddens both links and contrasts his approach to Beveridge. At the end of the chapter that presents his view of the role of the state, he proposes his alternatives to Beveridge's original Giants. Instead of Want, Giddens proposes autonomy; instead of Disease, active health; he replaces Ignorance with lifelong education; instead of Squalor, wellbeing; and in place of Idleness, initiative.

Giddens's presentation of alternatives to Beveridge's Giants is part of his approach to social policy that he calls positive welfare, and is also located in his wider social theory suggesting the need for increased reflexivity in the modern world (which Giddens calls 'late modernity', Giddens 1991b). Instead of identifying large-scale societal challenges, Giddens wanted to propose changes to the workings of the welfare system that would engage and support people in becoming more autonomous, by looking after their own health, being prepared to train and engage with learning throughout their lives, and taking the initiative in overcoming the challenges that they face. The role of the state, he suggested, was in putting in place infrastructure that supported people in these goals.

In his other work, Giddens acknowledges as least two challenges that appear to go beyond this approach to welfare – environmental degradation, and the role of financial globalization in shaping our lives – with both requiring international co-operation that is far beyond the scope of individuals to achieve. As such, Giddens' view of updating Beveridge is a combination of harnessing local initiative to achieve greater autonomy for people, with the state providing infrastructure that might support this, but with the state also dealing with major challenges that lie before us all. This first element, of harnessing local initiative, has a great deal in common with that of Cottam (2019), who, wanting to emphasize work from Beveridge that came after his 1942 Report, and based on localism and voluntarism, shows how a range of smaller-scale projects can respond more innovatively to help people than the more standardized and centralized approaches that welfare states often utilize.

Looking at this work, there are two main lessons – that political structures matter in the functioning of welfare (from Giddens' and Cottam's criticisms of what can become the deadening hand of centralized welfare) and that there is a need to be concerned with large-scale challenges – with the latter especially also perhaps matching the intention of Beveridge's original Giants, and providing a stronger basis for comparative research in the rest of the book.

A year after Giddens' book appeared, another key writer, Atkinson (1999) published a review considering what a 'Beveridge' in the 21st century might look like. Atkinson's short review presents three inter-related points. First, he makes the case for the integration of social and economic policy. Atkinson discussed changes to the economy since Beveridge's time, especially the shift from nationalization to a more privatized economy, and the remarkable changes to the labour market that have occurred, especially since the 1980s. Atkinson suggests that these changes mean that the government has far looser control of the economy than before, becoming a regulator than a direct participator. This means, however, that the government also has to take its regulation role far more seriously, especially with respect to areas of the economy that are crucial for us all, including rail regulation and pensions. Atkinson outlines an historical shift: Beveridge's report was part of a move to put in place a more interventionist governmental approach to economy and society, but Atkinson is suggesting that this might no longer work in the modern world (showing something in common with the critique of Giddens and Cottam).

Atkinson makes a second point that links back to one of Beveridge's central concerns – the importance of children. He suggests that the changing economy and society of the world today means that a dynamic conception of poverty is needed in which there is both a high turnover amongst low-income families, but also where declining social mobility means that some families may struggle to escape from poverty at all. However, even amongst families that are temporarily in poverty, its effects can be long-lasting, with poverty affecting diet, limiting educational opportunities, and leading to delay in accessing public services of all kinds, but especially healthcare. In this context, Atkinson stresses the importance of child benefit (also, as we have seen, a central concern for Beveridge), but also makes the case for a much stronger focus on child-based policies in other areas, with goods and services for children taking a much more central role in governmental reporting (and today, we might say, in terms of impact analysis).

Third, Atkinson calls for a new national minimum linked to citizen engagement with socially recognized activities. This would extend welfare-to-work programmes to embrace social need, and give new opportunities for people to make contributions in their own communities.

Finally, Atkinson calls for a much stronger international understanding of the welfare state in terms of its role in an increasingly globalized and interconnected world. Atkinson makes clear that, despite the decreased role of government he sees in the modern world, it is not a passive observer of globalization, with opportunities for countries to gain influence in bodies such as the European Union. Sadly, Britain's decision to leave the EU has meant that its influence in such debates is probably substantially reduced.

Atkinson, then, in line with Giddens and Cottam, appears to be pointing to the need to look at how political structures can change and adapt to deal with the challenges of the modern world, as well as re-emphasizing Beveridge's concern with the impact of poverty on children.

Beyond Giddens and Atkinson, a more recent updating of Beveridge's Giants comes from Danny Dorling, a committed and prolific author with deep concern about the challenges our world faces, and so clearly an important voice (Dorling 2019). Dorling's most explicit consideration of the Five Giants was published in 2015 (Dorling 2015); it does not present a straightforward one-for-one link with Beveridge's original Giants, but something more conceptual. Dorling framed his updating of Beveridge in terms of the series of beliefs that he suggests uphold social injustice through a process of 'duplicity' from institutions and governments that claim they are alleviating social problems, but which often maintain them or even make them worse.

The first false belief Dorling presents is that 'elitism is efficient'. He suggests this has a long history including IQ tests and other attempts to segregate society based on differences of one kind or another, and still underlies statistical systems such as those operated by the OECD. Dorling claims that dividing society up in this way, far from being efficient, instead increases inequality while preserving the status and position of those who gain most from the segregating systems.

The second false belief Dorling suggests is that 'exclusion is necessary'. He says this flows from the 'elitism is efficient' belief by showing that many people are excluded from normal social activities, especially as debt finance is increasingly needed to fund the necessities of life. Dorling suggests that, as workers are required to become more 'flexible' in terms of their employment contracts, and their rights and the representation of their rights through bodies such as trades unions diminish, the rich engage in increasingly extractive processes to maintain their income and wealth.

Dorling's third false belief is that 'prejudice is natural'; it gives the richest the justification of looking down on others, and is based on claiming that society is meritocratic, so that, if others are not doing well, that is due to their own failings. This, however, in Dorling's view, leads to a decline in respect and trust across society, as well as justifying the richest passing on their advantages in clearly non-meritocratic ways such as inheritance, as well as access to private education.

The fourth false belief is that 'greed is good' and this again justifies a form of capitalism in which the poorest may be lacking in access to basic societal infrastructure (including the internet, but also transport), while others have all the advantages that the presence of those factors brings. However, such advantages may also be a zero-sum game in which infrastructural advantages can impose a penalty on those without them – public transport users still have to deal with the pollution of vehicles they cannot afford, or sit waiting in the traffic jams to which car users contribute.

Dorling's final false believe is perhaps the most corrosive of all, and is 'despair is inevitable'. This is the belief that there is no escape from the situation outlined by the other four beliefs, and it explains the increased incidence of mental illness since the rise of neoliberal approaches to managing the economy since the 1980s.

We are left without much in the way of clear policy prescriptions from Dorling's analysis, but instead an imperative to act to challenge the false believes he identifies, and to reduce the inequality that results from them. Dorling expresses hope this will happen (despite his 'despair is inevitable' belief) as, to be blunt, he believes exploitation is now so widespread that there are few groups left to exploit further. Dorling also suggests that it would be harder to fool people because the beliefs he outlines were now showing to be so false, but, given that he wrote the book in 2015, so before the election of Trump and the UK Brexit vote, perhaps this might have been premature.

Giddens and Dorling took Beveridge as an inspiration for exploring the challenges facing the world now, and as an opportunity for rethinking our approach to welfare (Giddens) or for trying to explain how inequality is preserved (Dorling). The Royal Society of Arts, in a series of regional events for its Fellows in 2018, attempted to find out what the new Giants would be today.[1] By far the most popular answer was inequality, followed by a 'lack of connection', which was linked to isolation, loneliness and poor mental health. The third Giant was 'intolerance', linked to the election of Donald Trump as President and the UK Brexit vote because of the use of 'fake news' and populism surrounding those events. The fourth new Giant was 'apathy', linking to

Dorling's 'despair is inevitable' both in terms of tone, but also because of its association with mental illness. It is also worth reflecting that the widespread concern about these factors reflects the opposite of Giddens' hope for greater engagement and aspiration that might result from significant technological change.

The final new Giant was that of the environment, and linked to concerns about over-consumption and pollution, but where there were also opportunities related to conservation and to access to the countryside. This factor links back to Dorling's over-riding concern with the implications of greed.

If the views of Giddens, Dorling and the RSA are not representative of the public as a whole, then at the 70th Anniversary of the Beveridge Report, Ipsos MORI set out to find out what the public regarded as the major challenges facing the UK in November 2012 (Ipsos MORI 2012). The results were based on a national poll, and give yet another perspective on the challenges society faced at that time.

The biggest priority for the public in 2012 was the economy (55%) followed by unemployment (33%). Whereas unemployment fits clearly with one of Beveridge's original Giants, raising the economy as a concern was perhaps a factor of both the timing of the poll (four years after the global financial crisis, but still in an era where 'austerity' was regarded as a major concern), while also showing a general anxiety about the future economic situation. The possible reasons for this anxiety will be explored more in the next section, which considers the major changes to economy and society since 1942.

Beyond the economy and unemployment, the next biggest concern was the NHS (20%), followed by 'Race Relations and/or Immigration' (19%), Crime at 17%, Inflation at 16%, and then, linking more clearly back to Beveridge again, Education 14%, Poverty 13%, Housing 10% and Pensions/Security/ Benefits at 9%. These factors are a mix of concerns about welfare more generally (NHS, Education, Poverty, Housing, Pensions) with concerns about immigration (which can be seen as prescient in relation to the Brexit campaigns and vote) and the anxiety that comes from crime, despite most significant criminal offences being in significant decline by 2012, so pointing to a more general sense of anxiety in the modern world.

In 2012, nearly half (47%) of people gave support to raising benefits for the poor (even if it were to lead to higher taxes), but with 27% of people disagreeing. What is more interesting is that the gap between those supporting raising benefits was smaller than in the 1980s (55% to 22%), but much larger than it had been at the beginning of the financial crisis in 2008, when the two sides were more-or-less equal. However, 84% of people wanted strong means-tests for people claiming incapacity benefit, and 62% of people agreed that benefits should have a 'cap', especially for people who had 'too many children'. The theme of what we might call 'conditionality' in respect of benefits was further emphasized by 78% of people agreeing that people should lose some benefits if they turn down work.

In summary, looking at how others have written about the five Giants in more recent times presents us with a varied picture. Giddens's and Dorling's work provided contrasting approaches based on reconceptualizing the Giants, but with Giddens far more optimistic about the direction of travel in the modern world than Dorling. Atkinson shares with Dorling a more critical view of the contemporary world; and while his recommendations all seem positive, the reader is left to link them to the original Giants rather than explicit links being made. The RSA survey presents a range of concerns that contemporary society undoubtedly faces, but again they are not explicitly linked to Beveridge's original Giants, and are not linked to an explicit view of society. Finally, the Ipsos MORI poll may prove to be a product of its time, showing concern for the global financial crisis of 2008, but simultaneously showing continuing support for the welfare state, even if public support for social policy might be higher in times of greater economic insecurity.

Before we go further, however, we need to place these explorations of contemporary Giants in a wider context, as this will allow us to construct a framework for working out what the contemporary Giants the book will consider in Chapter 2 might be, as well as adding greater depth to the book by consolidating our knowledge of societal change over the last eighty years.

## CHANGES SINCE THE 1940S

We have now reviewed the Beveridge Report in its original context, outlining what some of the other writers who have called for an updated version of the Five Giants have said. Next, we must also think about how the world has changed since the 1940s in order to ensure that the book's approach encompasses the key contextual differences between then and now, and takes them into account in building its framework.

This section will consider both over-arching frameworks and individual factors for considering changes to economy and society over the last eighty years. With that in mind, a good place to start is with the work of Jessop, which is presented as key to debates around societal change in key social policy texts (Lister 2010), as well as serving as a strong introduction to the dimensions of change that we need to consider.

Jessop (1992, 1999, 2002) constructed a framework that is especially concerned with Anglo-American form of capitalism, but clearly has application beyond those countries as well. Jessop suggests that changes in the governance of welfare can be considered across four dimensions.

The first dimension is concerned with the shift from Keynesian macroeconomic management, seen as the dominant economic paradigm in the post-war period, but with Keynes's thought clearly being a significant influence on Beveridge in 1942. Keynesian macroeconomic management assumes a relatively closed national economy in which the government is able to intervene strongly in the running of the economy relatively free from concerns that international capital will leave the country or influence currency values should the government wish to pursue strategies that international money markets dislike. It also presumes that governments want to actively run their own economies, especially in terms of keeping unemployment relatively low (which was one of Beveridge's key assumptions).

Jessop suggests that Keynesian macroeconomic management gave way from the 1970s onwards to a new form that is based instead around what he terms 'Schumpeterian' policy, named after the economist Joseph Schumpeter. Rather than being concerned with managing the economy directly, the government's primary focus of control is on achieving international competitiveness. Its principal focus of economic policy moves from being concerned with its demand-side (a central part of Keynesian macroeconomic policy is the maintenance of demand by the government) to considering the supply-side instead, in which the government seeks to create an environment in which business can thrive in a more globalized world. As such, the government becomes less concerned with participating in the economy directly, and instead takes up a role where it attempts to provide a more supportive environment for business to do better. This means guarantees of full employment disappear, and a key concern for government policy becomes pursuing new economic orthodoxies by avoiding running large budget deficits and keeping low levels of inflation to avoid international capital flight in global financial markets.

Jessop's first change, then, is from government-managed macroeconomic policy in relatively closed economies, with the government intervening especially to maintain full employment (Keynesian macroeconomic management), to open economies in which the government aims to achieve international competitiveness and tries to prevent international capital outflows.

Jessop's second dimension of change is about social policy more directly, and involves a shift from 'welfare' to what he calls 'workfare'. Welfare is about the state providing services to people as a right of their citizenship, and clearly captures the aspiration of post-war policy as well as being central to Beveridge's Five Giants vision. Beveridge advocated for the state being much more responsible for meeting the needs of its people by putting in place a social security system (especially in terms of unemployment and pensions), creating a national health service and starting to pay family allowances to support children better. He also clearly regarded education and expanding the housing stock as crucial to post-war success, with the state taking the lead across these areas.

Jessop suggests that, again since the 1980s, there has been a movement away from welfare to what he calls, perhaps a little misleadingly, 'workfare'. Workfare, in Jessop's terms, is the subordination of social policy to other goals – especially economic growth. As such, welfare becomes more conditional on people making an economic contribution, typically through work. It is worth reflecting, however, that Beveridge was not in favour of rights-based unemployment benefits or pensions unless people were actively seeking work or taking training (for unemployment benefit) and did not want to pay out pensions for twenty years after his report in order for people to be able to pay into the social insurance fund first (he was over-ruled on this last recommendation as asking pensions to wait was not regarded as politically viable). Indeed, at least one updating of Beveridge's report (Saunders 2013) aims to emphasize the importance of personal responsibility and conditionality, which were very much present in the original publication.

Beveridge, then, clearly expected everyone to be contributors to the economy, even if the general direction of post-war welfare increasingly diverged from this vision. However, workfare goes one stage further than Beveridge's approach because social policy becomes increasingly seen by government as a cost or overhead to business. Keynesian macroeconomic policy regarded benefits as important not only to allow people to live, but also because they added 'demand' to the economy at times when economic slowdowns might be occurring. From a 'workfare' perspective, though, paying tax is a cost to business (and to individuals) that they might come to resent, perhaps interpreting themselves as paying for others to receive benefits when they are unlikely to receive much in return. This, in turn, can lead to a splitting of people between those who work and contribute, and those who do not. Such a view appears to be based on fundamental misconceptions of payments and receipts to the welfare state over our life-courses (Hills 2014), but it forms the starting point for political parties who wish to scale back welfare to make what seem to be electorally popular arguments about the need to reduce the taxation 'burden'. Taylor-Gooby (2013) captures this well in terms of a double-crisis: welfare services receive cuts, which make them less popular, which mean people demand more cuts, creating a potential downward spiral of funding and service levels.

Jessop's third change is around the scale of our economies and societies. He suggests we have moved from primarily national economies to ones that increasing are 'post-national'. Globalization is an important factor here, but this strongly relates to technical change as well (not least the internet, the explosive growth of which post-dates most of Jessop's work on his framework). As well as this movement 'upwards' resulting from globalization, and from the growth of international capital flows and trans-national corporations, governance forms have also seen movement away from the national state to more local levels (through processes of devolution and cities becoming stronger) as well as upwards with international bodies such as the World Bank becoming more important (especially for developing economies suffering difficulties). Trade blocs such as the European Union and NAFTA have come to take increasingly significant roles in the running of economies and societies. As such, the scale of governance is arguably far more complex than it was in the 1940s, with the different levels of governance being far more inter-linked and with the potential for events on the other side of the world to have far more impact on remote countries than was previously the case.

Jessop's final change is from what he calls 'state' to 'regime' form governance. This involves a shift in the post-war period where the state intervened in both industry and welfare services, to one where it has withdrawn, through processes of privatization in industry, and through increased use of partnership with the private and not-for-profit sectors, to a role where it attempts to co-ordinate rather than directly oversee. This shift has already been suggested in the work of Atkinson above, and is important as a dimension of change in its own right.

Jessop's four dimensions clearly overlap, and point to new forms of capitalism appearing in which the state has a very different role to the one it had in the 1940s and 1950s. The framework is not perfect, placing less of an emphasis on the importance of financial capitalism than is perhaps merited with the benefit of hindsight, which treats social policy through the lens of the labour market more narrowly than is ideal (Greener 2018). However, it does give us a strong basis for considering how the world has changed since Beveridge's time.

In addition to Jessop, two other writers (Beck and Giddens) have made significant conceptual contributions to our understanding that will be included here, and we will introduce a key concept, that of 'affluence', which also links to the discussion above in Jessop and Taylor-Gooby's work.

Beck's work set in train a series of research programmes from the 1990s onwards especially (Beck 1992), based on his work around the 'risk society'. Beck's thesis was that a major driver of societal change was the increasing scope of human activities to create new risks, both as we came to understand the world in greater scientific depth, but also as the potential for human action to change our world increased. Although we have also developed their potential, especially through the scientific lens, we do not necessary fully understand the implications or consequences of new-found technologies. In production, massive improvements in technology and transportation have created a global economy that has undoubtedly made most of us far richer than we would otherwise have been, but at the price of environmental damage that we did not foresee. New risks, such as climate change, require new solutions that we seem unable to deal with, especially as they require large-scale – probably beyond national – action. Global financial markets have created potential for the creation of extraordinary wealth, but they have also introduced risks around inter-linked crises – such as those of 2008 – that regulators did not appear to have foreseen.

Giddens, whose work we have already outlined, considers the world in similar terms to Beck, but through an arguably more optimistic lens. Giddens' work is especially important as he has, as we have already seen, contributed a new version of Beveridge's Giants framework, and that contribution is very much in line with his social theory (see especially Beck, Giddens and Lash 1994). Giddens shares concerns with Beck about global financial markets and environmental change, with the latter especially continuing to be a strong influence over his work (Giddens 2011). Giddens also raises concerns about how humans will cope with living in what he often refers to as a post-traditional world, in which the ideologies of the past have far less influence over us. However, within his understanding of modernity, especially what he calls 'late modernity' (Giddens 1991b), Giddens suggests that a more inter-linked world offers opportunities and what he calls 'reflexivity', in which people can reflect on the assumptions they hold about the world and come to understand it by using new ideas and concepts. Giddens hoped that technologies such as the internet would allow people to better understand what was going on in other parts of the world, and demand their governments adopt policies that work elsewhere. The internet, then, offers the potential for greater democratic accountability and for information to be more widely available to everyone, breaking free from the old gate-keepers of the past.

What is striking about Giddens' work, around twenty years on from the peak of its influence, is the extent to which he foresaw the direction of societal change that would appear in the coming decades. At the same time, the changes he predicted have also had a darker side. The internet can create a more informed citizenry and has been deployed to that end by the use of online petitions and the greater availability of information about governments. However, it has also of course led to a re-entrenchment of what can appear to be deeply regressive ideas in terms of attitudes to people from other countries as well as what we have come to call a 'post-truth' approach to knowledge, in which it can seem that anyone can make any claim they like, and well-grounded science can be challenged by conspiracy theorists (Fuller 2018). People can become more reflexive, but they can also retreat into 'bubbles' or 'echo chambers', where they only hear voices similar to their own, a far less healthy outcome.

Giddens, then, is important as he foresaw the direction of travel of major global challenges such as climate change and financial capitalism, but presented a more optimistic view of the future than did Beck. As such, Giddens' suggestions for updating Beveridge's Giants appear to be both located in his wider social theory, and perhaps optimistic compared to the world in 2022.

A third approach to understanding change since the 1940s brings together the work of Galbraith, Offer and Barber (B. Barber 2007; Galbraith 1958, 1993; Offer 2006) and is concerned with the implications of societies growing richer. Each of the three theorists has a different understanding of the consequences of this, but with some common themes.

Galbraith's work spanned half a century, and was directly concerned with the consequences of the changes he saw taking place and their likely future direction. In 'The Affluent Society', first written at the end of the 1950s (Galbraith 1958), Galbraith suggested that the focus of economic theory, concerned primarily with scarcity, was becoming less and less relevant as economies grew richer. Galbraith suggested that the basic needs of the population in developed economies were now being met, so industrial firms now had to engage far more in large-scale advertising that does not inform people of the existence of goods and services, but was fundamental in the creation of new needs it aimed to construct for them.

This creation of need through marketing has important consequences. It means that, as people become focused on private consumption, they come to neglect public services, resentful at their consumption being curbed by taxation, and to at least some extent many of the more affluent people becoming shielded from poverty by being able to separate themselves from it. We can see this where the rich and poor come to live in separate areas, or with the richest living in what we have come to call 'gated cities'. This results in what Galbraith calls 'private affluence and public squalor', with the potential for public services to become increasingly run down while the population, on average, but excluding the poorest, grows richer.

Galbraith revisited several of these themes in his later work, pointing to the growth in corporations that were largely insulated from business cycles by their ability to work across several markets and several countries (Galbraith 1975), and later in his life voiced his concerns about growing inequalities, over-dependence on financial markets for economic growth (about which he was often scathing), and of the 'culture of contentment' (Galbraith 1993) that extended this thinking in 'the affluent society' to raise concerns about the self-serving behaviours of those in power, but often supported by publics who themselves had escaped poverty and no longer wished to pay for services for those who had not. Similarly to Dorling (see previous section), Galbraith saw potential for change if those in power ran out of new groups they could engage in wealth extraction, but also feared that, if this did not occur, there was the potential for societal breakdown (Galbraith 1996). Galbraith's work is remarkable in seeing so early in the post-war period where the fractures and dangers facing capitalism were located.

Many of Galbraith's themes were later picked up by Offer, who, in *The Challenge of Affluence* (Offer 2006), deployed a range of datasets to look for changes in time over assets, income and wealth distributions, along with changes in demography, behaviour and psychological attitudes. Offer suggests that public decisions are becoming more myopic and short term, behaving as consumers in ways that satisfy their wants but, as a result, often running into debt and losing sight of the common good. This results in economic polarization, putting pressure on families who are continually pursuing consumer gains and having to pay off debt to support the lifestyles their consumption patterns require, and, at the extreme, even deciding not to have children because of their potential cost.

Offer, then, demonstrates with detailed empirical work that came substantially after Galbraith's claims, that many of his points appear to be strongly empirically supported. Offer, interestingly, does not cite Galbraith or seem aware of his work, but presents an argument with a great deal in common with it.

Finally, Barber (2007) argues that our growing consumerism is 'infantalizing' us, with mass marketing putting us on hedonistic treadmills where we are forever attempting to make ourselves happier through consumer purchases but where our purchases are instead leading to increased debt, to individualization, and to child-like behaviour where we are unable to delay gratification or engage in thought directed to the public good.

Barber's concerns echo those of Galbraith and Offer, but also link to another strand of Barber's work concerning the weakening of democracy (Barber 2004). Barber argues that democratic debate and deliberation offers us the opportunity to engage with those who share the spaces in which we live and find common ground, but our electoral, representative politics are moving us away from this, towards a more transactional model of democracy ('thin democracy') in which we simply vote without believing we have further democratic obligations. Barber argues that reinvigorating democracy requires far higher levels of deliberation and participation, and that we need to urgently reform our political processes towards those ends as it will lead to better political decision-making, but also act to counteract the individualization that results from the consumer society of which he is so critical. Barber's work is therefore prescient in being at the leading edge of theorists who have become increasingly concerned about the weakening of democratic life, and in combining that critique with the increasing consumerism of life, gives us a clear theoretical base for exploring the modern world. Galbraith, Offer and Barber then present a critique of the modern world as becoming overly dependent on mass advertising, consumption driven by debt, and individualization rather than the public good.

If we put together the insights gathered from the work reviewed above, we now have an outline of the factors that we have to take into account in constructing the criteria for the New Giants in the 2020s.

From Giddens and Beck, it is clear that globalization is a crucial factor, both in financial and cultural terms. Financial capitalism has grown massively, and the reach of multinational corporations into all our lives has been a major factor in changing the global economy. At the same time, Jessop points to the changes in governance that have resulted from globalization, with governments putting an increased emphasis on trying to move their economies to being more competitive rather than being concerned with demand-management, and seeking to reduce welfare rights to make them more conditional. As well as this, the range of organizations and institutions engaged in welfare has grown, with the state having to negotiate with large-scale trading blocs and world-level institutions upwards, and with increasingly powerful cities and regions below.

A second key theme in the work of Giddens, Beck, Galbraith and Offer is new risks and unintended consequences. Individual corporations, no matter how big, did not set out to cause global warming, but their actions in terms of polluting, but also in terms of creating mass consumerism, have clearly moved us in that direction. The new risks we face require large-scale co-operation beyond that capacity of even the largest individual states.

A third key theme comes from this second one, and is based around resistance to welfare (and even democratic processes) as we have become increasingly individualistic and consumer focused. In such an environment it is often difficult to make arguments for the public good, and this creates significant problems when trying to make arguments for the New Giants that we face.

The next section, starting with these themes, constructs a framework within which the book's New Giants will be located.

## A FRAMEWORK FOR CONSIDERING THE NEW GIANTS

We are now in a position to construct a framework that will allow the selection of the New Giants to be considered in this book. From the discussion above, the following appear as important criteria.

First, if the book is to make a link to Beveridge's Giants, each of the New Giants needs to be explained in relation to one of Beveridge's original selections. This is important as the book can then argue it is updating Beveridge's work in the spirit of his original thinking. This does not mean the New Giants have to be the same as Beveridge's original ones, but it does mean that each should be conceptually linked to one of Beveridge's original Giants. Without this conceptual link, there is a danger of the relationship to Beveridge's work not being clear.

Second, a clear theme of the section on changes since the 1940s is that the New Giants need to be global in scope. Beveridge was primarily concerned with the future of UK social policy and society, but, as we have seen, considering the UK by itself is no longer a viable strategy, the world is now far more inter-linked. At the same time, exploring how other countries are facing the Giants that the book will identify provides empirical evidence about the effects of different ways of governing social policy. In the same way as Beveridge sought to learn from what other countries were doing, so will this book.

Third, the book needs to be grounded in terms of what other explorations seeking to update the Giants have identified as the crucial challenges facing us all, while also taking into account the wider societal changes that have taken place since the 1940s and making sure they are incorporated. As outlined in the previous section, globalization, new societal risks (and their unintended consequences), and resistance to welfare are crucial factors that have to be recognized. There is certainly room for utopian thinking in welfare policy (Bregman 2017), but this book will be about finding what different countries have in common (and how they differ) in terms of the factors they already have in place.

Putting these criteria together, the book suggests that globalization is central to understanding changes to the world since the 1940s, and is also central to debates about welfare and its future (Hay 1998; Stiglitz 2003). This does not mean that global events had no impact in the 1940s – when Beveridge was writing his report a World War was taking place. What it does mean is that our economies and societies are far more inter-linked, and that those linkages are functioning far more quickly. The discussion above considered two aspects of this in particular. The first is financial globalization; this has led to the creation of an inter-linked financial network that has the potential to create vast investment opportunity, but also to cause financial chaos. The second aspect is cultural, and is another double-edged sword. An optimistic view (from Giddens) is that, as we become more aware of different ways of doing things in other countries, we can become more tolerant of difference, as well as demanding our own governments learn from the best practices in the world. A more pessimistic view is that there is a danger of our becoming more xeno-phobic and intolerant, with global news channels using their position to present nationalistic views and engaging in popularist rhetoric instead. Undoubtedly, we have seen both since the 2000s, but, in either case, the book will have to deal with the challenge of treating globalization seriously.

The discussion above has also outlined how the new risks that human activ-ity has caused and how these often lead to unintended consequences. The New Giants clearly have to take this concern into account. The example of environ-mental policy has already been raised, but another one related to the work of Galbraith is especially clear in the functioning of our labour markets. When we choose to purchase goods from the cheapest suppliers, we put downward pressure on other retailers for them to lower their costs as well. Retailers will look at a range of strategies, many of which may involve employing labour at cheaper rates or more flexible terms, and it is clear that this has led, in many countries, to workers having far fewer rights than they did thirty years ago. In some countries, greater flexibility has been negotiated with trades unions and introduced to try to benefit everyone (Thelen 2014); however, in other countries it has led to the growth of 'platform economy' jobs where substantial legal challenges have had to occur to allow even basic worker rights. What is important here is that our decisions as consumers can affect our lives as workers; the two are inter-linked, and if we do not consider both at the same time, we can't see the bigger picture of the decisions we make. If we purchase from retailers that seem to have found ways to avoid paying tax, we shouldn't be surprised to receive poorer public services.

Finally, there is the third key criterion for the New Giants – that of pragmatism. It is important that the New Giants work through what is possible in an environment of resistance to taxation and increased consumerism. By exploring how governance and societal factors combine to lead to better achievements in relation to each of the New Giants, we can see how these problems might at least be mitigated.

## WHAT IS MISSING?

I am acutely conscious that the discussion above has missed out two factors that are of central concern to social policy (and indeed, society) today – those of gender and ethnicity. Alongside the changes outlined above, the dynamics of gender relations have changed dramatically since the 1940s. Beveridge has been roundly criticized for the assumptions he made about the role of women in families (Williams 1989), and it would be ridiculous not to make clear that there remain significant challenges in addressing gender pay gaps (which persist, despite legislation dating back to the 1970s and even beyond), expectations about domestic and caring responsibilities, and the bane of domestic violence.

The countries of the world all still face significant challenges in respect of how they deal with racism, not helped by populist politicians in a range of different places engaging in crude, dog-whistle strategies to mobilize support for themselves. This behaviour is divisive and repulsive, and it is depressing that we have yet to leave these prehistoric attitudes behind.

Gender and ethnicity are serious subjects, and both could be presented as New Giants. I believe, though, that these issues require a different kind of analysis than this book aims to offer, as it is extremely difficult to do large-scale comparative analysis that engages at the depth they deserve. There is great work that has made huge strides forward in comparative understandings of gender (for example, Daly and Rake 2003), but I believe such treatments require full-length books in their own right, and including gender or ethnicity as Giants would end up masking much of the complexity that makes them so difficult to confront. It is crucial, though, to note that more work in these areas is desperately needed, especially exploring them comparatively, and I hope that researchers with expertise in them will take their work forwards towards that goal.

## CONCLUSION

This chapter has covered a lot of ground.

First, Beveridge's original Giants were outlined, putting them in the context of their own time, and explaining the importance of them in terms of the post-war welfare state. Next, we explored what authors who have sought to update Beveridge's Giants have suggested. We then moved on to consider societal changes that have occurred since the 1940s as a means of creating criteria for presenting societal challenges as New Giants. That section concluded by saying that, in order to be included as a New Giant, it had to be conceptually linked to one of Beveridge's original Giants, be global in scope, and take into account what other writers updating Beveridge's Giants have said. The New Giants will also involve collective action problems, so it will probably be beyond the scope of an individual government to deal with them, as well as to have empirical evidence available that measures them, to see what the countries that are doing the best in terms of each of the New Giants have in common.

The next chapter makes the case for each of the New Giants, some of which will be unsurprising because of their links to the discussion above, while others will be less obvious. Which New Giants will the book consider?

## NOTE

1. At https://www.thersa.org/blog/2018/07/britains-new-giants-your-verdict (accessed on 3 November 2021).

# 2.   The New Giants

## INTRODUCTION

This chapter provides an outline of the Beveridge Report in the context of its own time, exploring what a range of writers have suggested in terms of updating it, and constructing criteria for selecting New Giants. Subsequently it will make the case for five New Giants, which will form the basis of the empirical research in the rest of the book.

## NEW GIANT 1: FROM WANT TO INEQUALITY

In the language of Beveridge, 'Want' was primarily concerned with people who were unable to achieve a subsistence level of income. Alleviating Want was the main focus of the 1942 Report, and the primary means of achieving it, as proposed by Beveridge, was through the establishment of a social insurance scheme in which everyone would contribute at the same level, and in return be given the same right to claim the same unemployment benefits should they lose their job, or a pension when they reached retirement age. Beveridge's scheme was one based on contribution, and he made clear that people who had not contributed to the fund would instead receive social assistance (rather than social insurance), which would not be given as a right, but be linked to means-testing and a requirement, if necessary, to retrain (Beveridge 1942). This was because Beveridge wanted to make clear (and he believed the British people supported him in this) that people should not get 'something for nothing'. He also regarded unemployment not as permanent, but as an 'interruption' to work – and which he believed, based on pre-war surveys, to be the norm for nearly everyone. Beveridge also advocated that pensions not be introduced until people had contributed to a government-run social fund, which he wanted to be financially self-balancing and separate from other government spending. The fund would receive contributions from workers, employers, and the government at equal levels.

In Beveridge's proposals, benefits would be at subsistence levels only. He expected people to take out additional insurance should they want coverage beyond that level, making use of friendly societies to do so. Paying benefits at subsistence levels meant that people could afford to live (although differential levels of rents were a significant problem that he never really solved), and that everyone could afford to pay into the scheme at the same rate.

Relief from Want then, for Beveridge, came through everyone contributing to a social insurance fund, then, having done so, being able to draw unemployment benefit (if necessary) and pensions. Those who had not made contributions would face means-testing and, for unemployment payments, the possible need to retrain. The scheme was a little more complicated in terms of dividing people into 'classes', some of which worked in slightly different ways, but, for the most part, Beveridge's scheme was contributory, with flat-rate contributions and flat-rate benefits at subsistence levels.

The nearest equivalent to Want today is poverty. Our understanding of poverty today is somewhat different to that of Beveridge's time. A first useful conceptual split is between absolute poverty and relative poverty. Absolute poverty is close to the idea of 'subsistence' in the Beveridge Report, and is based on what someone needs to be able to have the very basics – food, water, clothing and shelter. If someone is unable to access these basics, we can say they are absolutely poor. It is therefore often unhelpful to attach a standard monetary level to absolute poverty, as the cost may vary considerably from one place to another. It is also the case that different places may make some of these basics more urgent than others – lack of access to shelter is more urgent in a climate that is cold and wet than in one that is drier and warmer, but in either case this is a necessity.

Relative poverty is, as the name suggests, less directly linked to the attainment of particular basics, but instead measured relative to the general standard of living in a country or place. The idea of the median income is useful here. The median income of a place is calculated by arranging all incomes in ascending (or descending) order, and then finding out which falls in the middle. This is different to the mean income, which is simply the total incomes in that place divided by the number of people. The median and mean incomes for an area are likely to be different because it is very possible there will be some people on very high incomes; this raises the mean income for everyone above that of the median level. If we want to try to represent the income of a place with a single number, the median is probably going to be a better measure. A standard benchmark used in the OECD is to find out what 60% of the median income is, and set that as the relative poverty threshold. This allows us to work out how many people have an income below that level, and find out the poverty rate as a result. At the time of writing this chapter, the highest poverty rate in OECD data is in Costa Rica at 0.199 (effectively 20%), followed by the United States at 0.178. To give some other comparisons, Spain is 0.142, Australia 0.124, the UK 0.117 and Germany 0.104, with the lowest rates being Finland 0.065, Czechia 0.061, Denmark 0.061 and the lowest in the dataset is Iceland with 0.049.[1]

Absolute poverty, then, gives us an indication of whether people can achieve the basics necessary for life, but is difficult to measure as the cost of those basics (especially shelter) vary from place to place. Relative poverty tells us about the distribution of income by giving an indication of how many people fall into the lowest earners in a place. It is easier to measure relative poverty, but, as the name suggests, it may not capture whether people actually have access to the resources they need.

Despite the continuing importance of absolute poverty, income levels (at least on average) have risen significantly since Beveridge's day. We now take for granted a range of goods and services that would have been deemed luxuries in the 1940s, when only around half of households in the UK had both hot water on tap and an indoor toilet. Many of my generation's parents talk about the hazards of outdoor toilets, especially at night-time in the winter, and, in their childhoods, of the need to boil water on the stove in order to have a bath (the water they had to inherit should older siblings also need to bathe). We have to bear in mind changing standards of living when considering poverty. Absolute poverty remains with us, but it has become increasingly important to consider poverty from the relative perspective.

Relative poverty matters not only because, if we are to live in a society in which we treat one another with respect then there is a need to care about the plight of others, but also because societies with greater levels of inequality appear to have more health and social problems (Wilkinson and Pickett 2010). Those directly affected by poverty are likely to live shorter lives with higher levels of stress. They are likely to have less self-determination or say in the way that their lives go, and have access to less meaningful work (if they are able to find work). However, they are also likely to be subject to 'status syndrome' (Marmot 2012), as they will find themselves, upon comparing their lives with those of others with more resources, to be falling short (Frank 2007).

People who are living in poverty will have fewer resources with which to navigate their lives, suffering the strain of not being able to cope in the face of a financial emergency of one kind or another (often in the United States related to health care costs, Schneider et al. 2017). They therefore come to live with a level of background stress where they know that, should anything go wrong, the only answer they might have is to take on additional debt, and with a range of lenders offering punitive rates of interest widely advertising their services. In these circumstances, people may be less able to cope with 'normal' problems because of the lack of money. Ground-breaking research from Mullainathan and Shafir (2013) showed that the level of strain this can lead to is equivalent to sleep deprivation.

Undoubtedly being in poverty increases the strain of day-to-day living, and it can bring additional challenges. Perhaps having to juggle more than one job, people may find themselves living in areas with lower rents but with less access to good-quality food because housing is further away from mainstream stores (Butler 2017). There may be higher crime levels in some poorer areas, adding further to their burden. On top of all of this, people living in poverty may find themselves being branded in the media as feckless or as 'scroungers' should they claim benefits to try to subsist.

The labelling of people claiming benefits as 'scroungers' shows a profound lack of understanding of both the workings of the welfare state, and of ways in which the world of work has changed. Over the course of our lives, the vast majority of us receive back from welfare services the overwhelming majority of the payments we make into them (Hills 2014). Taxation is less a transfer to others, than a kind of individual public services savings account of our own, but one in which those who are better off are more likely to pay in more than they receive back, and those who are worse off draw more than they contribute. However, everyone receives benefits of some kind in their receipt of public services. Equally, the world of work has changed dramatically (which we will pick up later in this chapter), with the clear line between those in full-time per-manent work, contributing taxation, and those out of work receiving benefits, now becoming far more blurred. The way that work is organized, the contracts we work to, and the levels of pay for many people, have undergone significant changes.

For some writers (Frankfurt 2015) poverty is inextricably an absolute concern only – once people have reached subsistence level, it should not be their concern how others are living. In this view, we should be satisfied with our own lives and get on with living. However, this view seems to overlook the research outlined above that those in lower 'status' positions in society, because of their lower levels of self-determination, also have higher levels of stress and suffer a range of health effects as a result.

It also seems to be the case that, in societies with higher levels of inequal-ity, not only are the poorest more likely to struggle, but this leads to lower levels of social cohesion and trust across all social groups. This lack of trust and social cohesion is likely to lead to higher rates of a range of social ills (Wilkinson and Pickett 2010), which will cause strain on everyone who has to live with them. We can see a direct link here with the work of Barber and Offer explored in Chapter 1, whereby, as societies grow more unequal, they become more individualized, less concerned with the public good, and more consumer-driven; and more people find themselves aware that they are falling short of the income and consumption patterns of those who are the best off. Again, it is possible to argue that what others earn or how they live shouldn't matter so long as everyone has enough to be able to live. But this ignores the fact that humans are social creatures, who necessarily compare what they have to others. In more consumer-driven societies, people's identities will be increasingly shaped by what they wear, where they live, what job they have, and a range of other factors that serve to differentiate between them, and in which a large number of people risk finding themselves, unless they are prepared to take on debt or work across several jobs, both of which are additional sources of strain, falling short. Higher inequality therefore, as it turns out, isn't just worse for the poorest, but probably for everyone.

As such, this book treats inequality as the first of the 'New Giants'. This is justified in the discussion above, in terms of the shift of concern from absolute to relative poverty, but also in terms of the increasing evidence that relative poverty is a problem for everyone in such a society, not the poorest alone. Inequality is clearly conceptually linked to poverty, and so to Want, one of Beveridge's original Giants.

Inequality also meets the criteria for being a New Giant in that it is also an international problem; it is not isolated to particular countries or regions (Picketty 2014). Global inequality has become a major focus of comparative research, and this provides us with a rich range of existing work to draw from. Inequality is also a collective action problem, as none of us (I hope) sets out to create a society with greater levels of inequality, even if some economists would argue that some degree of inequality is necessary in order to incentivize people to try to achieve social mobility (a sentiment that Beveridge might have shared). There is some sense here – we all need to be motivated to improve life for ourselves, our family and those we care for. However, in doing so, we often cause dysfunctional consequences for others, as many of the goods that we try to attain are relational and limited in supply. Those of us who are parents and well off try to send our children to the best schools we can, perhaps paying private fees or buying a home near a good school, but these options may be unavailable to poorer families. We try to advise our children to attend the best schools or universities, or make use of our own social links to find our children work, giving them access to knowledge and networks that other families lack. We vote for political parties offering us tax cuts so we can keep more of the income that we earn, but this can lead to lower benefit rates for poorer families, poorer public services and increased inequality as there is less redistribution through the taxation system occurring. We engage in consumerism, trying to buy goods that others cannot afford and often displaying those goods as part of our identity, but at the cost of excluding those who cannot afford them.

In terms of the third criteria for being a New Giant, there are internationally accepted measures of inequality that allow us to look across the world and explore which countries appear to be more or less unequal. Achieving a lower level of inequality is not utopian. Some countries have much lower levels of inequality than others, while at the same time having thriving economies and rich societies. We can learn from them.

In summary, absolute poverty is still with us, but at nowhere near the level it was in 1942. There is increasing evidence that we need to focus on relative poverty, and that leads to a need for us to address levels of inequality. Inequality is linked to a range of social ills including poorer health, not just for those in poverty but for everyone in poorer societies. It is the first of the New Giants that this book will explore.

## NEW GIANT 2: FROM DISEASE TO PREVENTABLE MORTALITY

Disease was a significant concern for Beveridge not only in its own terms, as in the early 20th century the range of treatments that had been newly developed, including the antibiotics used widely in World War 2, were simply unavailable, but also because of the difficulty many people had in achieving access to healthcare at all.

The development of medicine as a profession is a fascinating story in its own right (Abbott 1988; Freidson 1988). In its early days, systems of medical understanding were based on the third-century works of Galen, and doctors may have done at least as much harm as good through practices such as bleeding, the administration of toxic substances as medicines, and surgeons' lack of belief in basic hygiene. Le Fanu (1999), in his 'long-sweep' accounts of the development of medicine, shows how these beliefs were gradually transformed (often in the face of significant resistance from organized medicine) into a form that began to incorporate empirical studies, and where practices were updated. War was a crucial element in the improvement of surgery as doctors worked on or near frontlines and innovated in the face of the terrible injuries they saw. Medical research began to expand to take into account new drugs, with penicillin being used in World War 2 to considerable effect. Perhaps less obviously, war was also a spur in states' realizing the extent of their populations that were unfit to be soldiers (Winter 1980), which led to calls for action to address this problem.

Once basic public health infrastructure has been built, improving the quality of water and putting in place sewerage systems, gaining access to healthcare for those in work was the next priority for state intervention, with the government underwriting costs or offering tax incentives for employers to support their workforce in receiving care. However, those not in work often had to rely upon charity. In the UK, GP surgeries would have a front door (for paying patients) and a back door (at which those without the resources would queue, and be seen if the doctor were willing).

In addition, healthcare also has some important characteristics that make it of special importance. Good and bad health is partially under our control, through our lifestyle choices, but disease and ill-health can also fall on those who have led relatively blameless lives. We may never smoke, yet still develop lung cancer. Understandings of the causes of disease have also

changed dramatically. In the post-war period, many people smoked because
it was a popular practice, and there was, to start with, no clear understanding
of its being damaging to health. Evidence about diet and exercise has changed
considerably over the last twenty years (see Taubes 2008, for example). Our
genetic inheritance (over which we have of course no control) can play a significant role in our susceptibility to disease. We can be genuinely doing our
best to look after ourselves, but simply be unlucky and need medical help.

When we do need healthcare, it is likely to be expensive. Doctors are
(rightly) highly trained, and their services do not come cheaply. Drugs may
have taken years to develop, and even if their ingredients are not expensive, the
final products can end up costing a great deal. The infrastructure and facilities
required for significant surgery can be enough to bankrupt even financially
comfortable families if they have to find the money to pay themselves – and
in countries like the United States, where there are often still significant 'gaps'
in health coverage for people, meeting medical expenses remains a significant
source of financial trouble or bankruptcy (Schneider et al. 2017).

It is also the case that, even if we can access treatment, disease can lead to
long-term health problems, both physical and mental. These long-term health
problems, in turn, can lead to a loss of income, or even a permanent loss
of work. In the context of the COVID-19 pandemic, the existence of 'long
COVID' may lead to our living with the effects of the pandemic for years after
effective vaccines have been introduced.

As noted in the previous section on Want, it is also the case that disease
generally falls more on the poor than on the rich because of the additional
strains of both living with poverty as well as the increased likelihood of
reduced-quality housing, an increased chance of being subject to crime, and
with poor-quality, low-cost food being available in abundance. Moralistic
claims about the cheapness of vegetables miss the point that, in many places,
they are not easily available via public transport, and often require more time
to prepare – a key factor if you are trying to work across several jobs. We also
know that smoking rates are higher amongst the poorest in society, and this
reflects an additional health risk.

Healthcare raises profound equity issues. If a healthcare system is organized
on the basis of people paying for the services they need, the poorest may not
be able to afford to receive care. If the government pays, there will always be
concerns that people are not taking sufficient responsibility for looking after
themselves ('moral hazard', as economists refer to this problem, Mooney
2003). If we use a mix of funding sources (both public and private), finding
a fair balance can be difficult – we want people to be able to access healthcare
when they need to, with some groups (young men, for example) often reluctant
to engage with doctors even when they need to. Health research, especially
with regard to new pharmaceutical treatments, can be coming up with new

drugs and treatments, and governments cannot afford to pay for them all. There needs to be a process by which hard decisions are made about what governments might pay for, and what treatments remain accessible for private payment only, but that will again leave those unable to afford such treatments feeling unfairly treated.

Achieving wider access to healthcare was a gradual process, and has still not been fully achieved in some developed countries. In the United Kingdom, Beveridge realized that World War 2 was an event that focused people's minds on what the world could be like in the future, and which he mobilized in his visionary language. Beveridge did not specify what kind of health service should be introduced in the United Kingdom, but he was clear that people needed better access to healthcare, and that it should be available to everyone.

Chapter 1 outlined the huge changes to economy and society since 1942. Healthcare has also changed massively in that time period. It is now far more expensive, and absorbs far more of our national income than it did then. In the UK, even during World War 2, healthcare was around 1% of national income. In the 2020s, it is around 10% – and the United Kingdom is very much at the lower end of healthcare spending compared with other large economies (OECD 2017b).

This massive increase in spending is due to a range of factors. Medicine has increased massively in scope, covering a far greater range of conditions. Medical research has grown more sophisticated and complex, producing drugs and technologies that are far more expensive than those available in the 1940s. Persons working in healthcare are far more highly trained, with that training costing more, and the resulting professionals need to be rewarded for their skill and expertise. Hospitals have become increasingly high-technology, requiring greater investment and upkeep. We have become increasingly aware of the importance of mental health, and now fund a far wider range of services than was previously the case. All of these factors have contributed to healthcare increasing in cost.

As developed economies have increased their expenditures on healthcare, those costs have become more and more politically salient. If countries are to spend 10% of their national income (or much more) on healthcare, and the state is going to have a significant role in funding that care, governments have wanted to be far clearer about what they are getting in return, and to try to ensure value for money is being achieved. This has resulted in governments putting in place a more active approach to healthcare management than was the case in the 1960s and 1970s, with the use of performance management and the extension of information systems to measure healthcare activity and outcomes far more closely to try to improve their performance. Both approaches have been controversial (Bevan and Hood 2006; Greener 2005).

At the same time as more and more money is spent on healthcare, however, it has also become clearer that health is too important to leave to healthcare systems alone (Bambra 2017). As well as simple luck, many of the factors that have important influences over our health are social – where we live, what our job is, even our ethnicity in the context of the place in which we live and work. These factors often inter-link with our health behaviours and access to healthcare to create complex patterns of cause and effect. It remains the case, though, that where you live is a significant determinant (on average) of how long you will live (Commission on the Social Determinants of Health 2008).

Putting all of these factors together means that health and healthcare remain a significant challenge today, in terms of accessing the healthcare we need, in terms of our own lifestyle choices, in terms of the cost of care, and in terms of a range of social factors that have an influence on our health. These factors have combined during the COVID-19 pandemic in debates over who should have priority access to vaccines, how particular groups may not wish to be vaccinated, how a range of factors (especially age and obesity) increase the likelihood of becoming seriously ill with the virus, and how a range of living conditions and practices combine with increased virus transmission. We have rearranged our lives, with many of us working from home, but others being expected to deliver goods to our door – and so perhaps taking greater risks with their own health.

'Disease' defined in broad terms, remains with us, especially in an age that is witnessing a generation-defining pandemic. How can we capture the discussion above in defining a New Giant?

What appears to conceptually link the cost of healthcare, access to it, the role of luck in our lives, and the challenge of dealing with disease more generally (including viruses) is what the OECD calls 'preventable years of life lost'. This idea attempts to capture and weight deaths that occur at younger ages, many of which may be preventable, in order to be able to consider which countries are managing to prevent such deaths, and which are not. This not only means treating disease in a more inclusive way than medical care alone; it also tries to capture how different countries are trying to enable people to be healthier for longer. In the OECD measure, age 70 is used as the cut-off point (a conservative measure, as many developed nations have life expectancies considerably high than this).

The point here is that medical care can do incredible things, but such extraordinary treatment is not available to everyone, and there are key factors affecting our health that go well beyond medicine. There is little point in our being able to treat diseases if people with those diseases cannot access care, a key factor in Beveridge's requirement for a national health service in the 1940s. In general, treatments must be available for everyone, or we discriminate against some groups. But healthcare alone does not account for preventable mortality.

Within the same basic geographic areas, neighbourhoods can differ significantly in terms of life expectancy, despite everyone having access, at least in principle, to the same health services. Considering preventable mortality in terms of the lives lost before the age of 70, and comparing nations gives us a way into looking at these discrepancies, and an opportunity for learning. Rather than focusing on disease, we need to take a wider view and be more concerned with avoidable death. We need to find what mix of factors appears to best achieve this, while at the same time not so over-burdening societies with the costs of healthcare that other social problems face funding reductions.

Preventable mortality meets the criteria we set out for inclusion as a New Giant, being conceptually linked to Beveridge's Giant of Disease, but reconceptualizing it in terms of the progress made by modern medicine, and also taking into account some of the challenges in terms of access, cost and social determinants. Preventable mortality is global in scope, varying significantly from country to country, and making comparisons between those countries gives us the opportunity to consider which are doing best, and what they have in common. Preventable mortality also reflects a collective action problem, as many of the factors underlying it result from individual decisions about health and lifestyle that we may make for the best of reasons, but which result in creating a context where things are worse for others. Our individual decisions about health and lifestyle, as well as the choices we make about where to live, and about doing our best for our own children to have a good start in life, all have health consequences for others. Finally, preventable mortality can never be reduced to zero, but looking to countries that do (badly) use this measure gives us an opportunity to form evidence-based comparisons that can enrich us all. As such, rather than disease, this book will focus on a second New Giant, that of preventable mortality.

## NEW GIANT 3: FROM IGNORANCE TO THE CRISIS OF DEMOCRACY

It is worth giving some context in relation to how different education was in 1942, and why Beveridge regarded it as being so important. In the UK in 1938, around 80% of children left school at age 14, which was also the age at which compulsory schooling ended. Children leaving education at age 14 often remained at primary school (rather than moving into secondary education). There was a belief that the extension of the school age to 14, which occurred at the end of World War 1, had improved social mobility. A planned expansion of higher education between the wars, however, had not occurred on affordability grounds. There was a faith in testing as a means of 'sorting' children, and moving them into forms of schooling that would best meet their needs (see Chitty 2004, Timmins 2017 for longer assessments of the situation in the 1940s).

The UK's 'Butler' Act of 1944 (after the Minister of Education who constructed it) addressed the need to improve education further, putting in place compulsory free secondary education and raising the age of school leaving to 15 (it was not until the 1970s that it was raised to 16). The major challenges Butler faced was one around the role of faith-based education and private schooling, and he found compromises on both that shaped the post-war UK education system. State schools were split into grammar schools (generally regarded as the best secular schools, but which required the passing of a test at age 11 for admission), secondary modern and technical schools, which were meant to have a stronger vocational element. There was a clear sense in government of these representing 'gold', 'silver' and 'bronze' children, which proved difficult to change (Timmins 2017). Labour removed the three-way education split in the mid-1960s, creating comprehensive schools to try to overcome the distinctions made within the system (and the prejudices they led to). However, whether or not these new schools led to education improvements remains a contentious issue (Ball 2017; Chitty 2004). Both grammar schools and private schools remained, undermining the attempt to give equal access to the same kind of education for everyone.

Compulsory schooling until age 15 meant that literacy rates improved in the UK, but significant challenges remained in terms of a comparatively weak offering for vocational education, despite numerous attempts to reorganize further and higher education especially (Thelen 2014). There was also a sense that British education was lagging behind that of its industrial competitors, leading to the establishment of a national curriculum to attempt to standardize provision to a greater extent in the 1980s (Chitty 2004) and to the widespread use of targets and league tables in the 2000s (M. Barber 2007).

In the 2020s, education is meant to serve a wide variety of purposes. There is clearly an emphasis on two roles, but with the possible neglect of a third, which will form the basis of the New Giant in this book. The first role of education, often clearest in policy documents, is to prepare people for work. This is clearly crucial, as education needs to give people the skills they will need in their lives in order to get work and function in the wider economy. If we were to educate people in a way that did not help prepare them for work, this would be perverse. In a world that is changing more rapidly, there is increasingly an emphasis on 'learning to learn', or acquiring not only skills, but also the meta-ability to acquire new skills as the world changes. This links to a focus on the need for lifelong education, rather than expecting people to acquire all the skills they need by 16, 18 or 21.

The second purpose of education is based around becoming a member of society. Although much parodied and complained about, education is a key part of how we learn about the world in which we live. We learn our country's history, a subject that has become more controversial as more critical approaches to dealing with the past have emerged that have asked questions about colonialism and sexism and have suggested that those we have often reified as great leaders may also have had significant personal faults. Those seeking to preserve tradition are often hostile to this newer approach, and there is a significant challenge in trying to find ways of narrating the story of our country, and taking pride in its accomplishments, while at the same time acknowledging both faults and the impact our own country might have had on others, as well as on marginalized groups in our own societies.

The third purpose of education arguably straddles the two already listed. As well as being workers and members of our country, we are citizens. In the 2020s, it seems that this role is in danger of being 'squeezed' out by the other two (especially in relation to the need for work-based skills) at the same time as the dangers of that happening are growing.

Education plays crucial roles in providing work-based skills or in integrating us into society. A more educated workforce should be more productive, helping raise the standard of living for everyone. Making sure people understand their own country and its past is also hugely important (and not separate from the citizen role, as we will see). However, it is also crucial that the citizen role is not lost because of the clear implications this appears to be having around the functioning of our democracies.

The claim that our democracies are in a crisis of one kind is becoming increasingly commonplace. This can be illustrated by Google's Ngram Viewer, which shows the incidence of the combination of the term 'crisis of democracy' in books, and which produces the following (at 22/5/21).

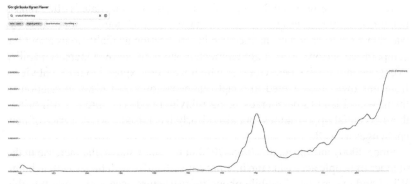

*Figure 2.1      Google Ngram for 'Crisis of Democracy'*

The chart above has a peak in the 1930s, as the Great Depression led to the questioning of governments worldwide, peaking in 1940 as the world entered war. From there, the curve flattens though the 1960s, but then begins a steady rise to 2000, when it reaches the 1940s levels, followed by an explosive increase in the 2010s. There appear to be several explanations being proposed for what has happened.

A first explanation, concerned with the steady rise of the curve from the 1960s to the 2000s, is linked to the rise of consumerism and individualism in the post-war period. A society based increasingly on the production and consumption of mass consumer goods has been linked to a decline in collective forms of public behaviour, perhaps captured most comprehensively in the US context by Putnam, in his work on the decline of 'social capital' (Putnam 2001). Putnam suggests that the decline in participation in a range of civic associations leads to a further decline in political involvement, reduced voter turnout, as well as increased distrust in organized politics. There are clear links with work already outlined from Galbraith and the 'culture of contentment' as well as with Offer and his view of 'affluence' and Barber and his concerns about 'thin democracy'. The suggestion is that, as we grow more affluent, we become less inclined to take an interest in the public good, and more concerned with pursuing our own interests. In an environment of mass advertising, consumption becomes our main interest, and we become less used to the compromise and negotiation involved in trying to do political work as we are used to getting our own way through a simple purchase (or decision not to purchase) in a market-driven environment (Baldock 2003). In such an environment, political life is reduced to a periodic public vote, rather than people being more actively engaged or involved in any kind of civic or political association.

If these accounts try to explain what has happened up to 2000, the explosive increase in concerns about the state of democracy after that date is often linked to the rise in internet usage. As we saw in Chapter 1, Giddens's hope (in 1998) was that a combination of the increase in information available to us about the comparative performance of government, along with our own increased ability to engage in reflexive behaviour, in which we were exposed to different views from our own, and learned to adapt our behaviours and ideas in relation to them, would lead to democracy being reinvigorated. The internet still brings these potential opportunities, but also clearly has raised a whole series of new challenges as well.

Since 2000, and especially 2005–2010 in the chart above, the increase in the number of people accessing the internet conveniently (with the growth in home Wi-Fi and expansion of mobile phone infrastructure access meaning that this is done through devices such as smartphones or tablets as much as computers), along with the massive growth of online social media platforms, has meant many of us spend far more time online. These platforms can be sites of learning and genuine exchange, as Giddens hoped, with classic examples showing how people have used social media to organize democratic protests or communicate with one another in oppressive regimes. Another classic example is the growth of free-to-use software that is the result of massive online collaborations of people who, in turn, give their time to collective projects with the development of Linux (in all its forms), Python and Wikipedia all showing the collective potential of such massively collaborative processes.

However, the massive increase in online activity since 2000 has also had significant downsides. Unregulated social media communications have become sites where bogus or fraudulent news stories can freely circulate, leading to the creation of terms such as 'post-truth' and 'fake news'. Voices that were previously excluded from having a public presence because of their extremism have found ways of communicating to new audiences, expanding their reach. People who are leaders in their fields and try to use social media to communicate research findings, often find themselves receiving abuse, and even threats to their lives. This seems especially the case where those experts are women. Politicians using social media are now regularly abused in the vilest ways. Social media has allowed people to 'filter' (Pariser 2012) their worlds so that they do not see views other than the ones they hold – even national broadcasters such as the BBC allow us to add settings to news web-sites so that we don't see stories outside a limited range of areas. All of this is a considerable distance from the world Giddens imagined back in 1998.

Many of these elements seemed to come to a head in 2016 with the election of Trump as president, based on the propagation of short slogans endlessly repeated via social media and in campaign rallies such as 'Build the Wall' (for a wall between the US and Mexico) and 'Lock Her Up' (concerning allegations against Trump's opponent, Clinton). Trump himself went on to become president, with the media becoming so used to him making misleading statements that they simply stopped reporting them. The *Washington Post*'s 'fact-checker' reported that Trump made over 30,500 misleading statements while in office.

The year 2016 also heralded Brexit in the UK, in which the lack of trust in politics and of politicians became very clear. The Conservative govern-ment sent out a brochure to every household in the UK outlining the case for remaining in the EU, but the 'Vote Leave' campaigns countered with emotive television advertising, a 'battle bus' claiming that leaving the EU would 'save' the UK £350M per week (which could be spent on priorities such as the NHS), and billboard posters that were thinly disguised attempts to raise concerns about immigration. A pro-EU MP was murdered during the campaign. After a campaign that showed the lack of trust in political leaders of all colours, the UK voted to leave the EU by a narrow majority, putting UK politics on a trajectory of conflict that remains with us five years later (Shipman 2016).

The crisis of democracy is therefore the third of our New Giants. It is linked to Beveridge's Giant of Ignorance in that it highlights the importance of education not only in terms of providing skills for work, or integrating us into society, but in the flourishing of our civic life, something that appears to be significantly under threat. Although the examples given above come from the US and UK, the crisis of democracy is global in scope: we have seen the rise of far-right groups across Europe and, at a global level, the 2018 Economist Intelligence Unit Report[2] explored the different dimensions of global democratic problems showing the challenges go far beyond Europe and America.

The crisis of democracy also reflects a collective action problem. Many of us sense that something has gone very wrong over the last thirty years in particular, with traditional political allegiances breaking down and becoming more complex, and decreased trust in our politicians. The extraordinary behaviours visible on social media every day show we face considerable problems in our civic lives. However, how we deal with all of this appears to be beyond our individual capacities. Chapter 6 will explore which countries, however, appear to be doing better than others. By gathering empirical data and looking at the patterns of factors that countries with stronger democratic institutions seem to have, we can move beyond utopian thinking, which can be a problem in democratic theory, and look at concrete examples of countries that do this best. We can then look to see what we can learn from them.

## NEW GIANT 4: FROM IDLENESS TO JOB QUALITY

In the 1940s, the next of Beveridge's original Giants, Idleness', is most closely linked to unemployment, and was an area where Beveridge held considerable expertise. Before World War 1 he was a campaigner for a national system of what were then called 'labour exchanges', where job vacancies and those out of work could be matched against one another (Harris 1998). Pre-World War 1, Beveridge appeared to regard unemployment as an example of market inefficiency (Beveridge 1909), and this informed his thinking when he was invited by Churchill to join the Board of Trade, where he was given the opportunity to set up his labour exchanges as a means of combatting both unemployment and poverty.

Between the wars, Beveridge became director of the London School of Economics, as well as serving on a range of governmental committees. His views on unemployment changed considerably (Harris 1998). First, there was the Great Depression during which it was hard to argue that unemployment was simply a matter of the better availability of information for jobseekers. Beveridge began to think again about the causes of unemployment and the role of government in the economy. Second, it is also the case that Beveridge was increasingly in touch with Keynes during the 1930s, the time in which Keynes was constructing and popularizing his *General Theory of Employment, Interest and Money* (first published in 1936), and which pointed to 'demand-deficient' unemployment and the need for government to take action in the circumstances in which it arose (Keynes 1997).

During World War 2, he was invited back into government, but not in as extensive a role as he would have liked (Beveridge wanted to oversee wartime manpower). Beveridge was allowed to carry out some manpower surveys, which made recommendations in 1941, but did little to ingratiate himself with Ernest Bevin (Harris 1998); and so, when the opportunity to move Beveridge to what appeared to be a minor committee reviewing social insurance, Bevin did so. As outlined above, Beveridge used this opportunity to compile his 1942 report.

If Want was the main focus of the Beveridge Report, Idleness was clearly linked to it, and also takes up a substantial part of the report. Beveridge presented a view of the subject compiled over thirty years of his own research and involvement in government. It is worth outlining the general principles that appeared in the report to consider how (and if) they apply today.

First, unemployment was considered predominantly an 'interruption' to work. This seems an unusual claim given the mass unemployment of the 1930s, but it was based on a range of surveys that had taken place pre-war, and which Beveridge poured over in detail. Given unemployment was an interruption, the question came of how people could be helped during such employment breaks.

Second, Beveridge believed strongly that people should be contributing to the economy, and that, if people were to receive unemployment benefits as a right, they needed to have paid into a social fund first. There were exceptions (amongst Beveridge's 'classes' of people) to this rule, but this was his general principle. Unemployment benefit was conceptualized by Beveridge as a form of social insurance, and he claimed that the vast majority of British people supported him in the view that people should only receive it as a right if they were contributing as well.

Third, Beveridge was fully aware that some people would not have paid into a social insurance scheme – what would become of them? For people who had not contributed to social insurance at the required level (spelt out in some detail in the report, and in relation to the 'class' of people to which you belonged), Beveridge allowed for the existence of social assistance. However, he made clear that social assistance should be inferior to social insurance, in that it would be means-tested and have training-based conditions attached to it if people were consistently unable to find work – especially for younger people.

Fourth, Beveridge wanted everyone to both pay into social insurance and receive benefits from it, at the same 'subsistence' rate. Unemployment, through social insurance, should be enough to live on, but no more. This was necessary because Beveridge wanted everyone to contribute at the same rate (meaning that the overall pool of money would be based on what the poorest could afford to pay in), but also because he felt that those who wanted benefits above subsistence levels should take out additional insurance through friendly societies. Although Beveridge was scathing of the inefficiency of friendly societies in paying out basic-level benefits (hence the need for his government-based scheme), he believed that they could have an important role in providing higher levels of insurance for those who both wished to, and could afford to pay for it. Beveridge's social insurance scheme then, was flat-rate (in terms of both contributions and benefits), conditional on people having paid in at the appropriate rate (if they wanted benefits without means-testing or possible training requirements), and payable at subsistence levels only.

There was also at least one clear problem with the scheme, of which Beveridge was fully aware. That issue was the housing costs. There is an extensive discussion in the report as to how differential 'rents' should be taken into account, but without real resolution. Beveridge suggested an average level of rent could be incorporated into social insurance, but this did not solve the problem, as he admitted himself. He was left hoping that a post-war home-building programme might alleviate shortages and even out rental payments. This issue of how to deal with differential housing costs remains very much with us today, especially in the more popular cities of the world where it is genuinely unclear how those on lower incomes are able to live (this will be revisited in relation to the Giant of 'Squalor' below).

As outlined in Chapter 1, the labour market has changed significantly since the 1940s. Between the 1940s and 1970s, unemployment remained relatively low in most industrial economies, fuelled by the post-war boom based on mass production and consumption (a growth wave known as 'Fordism' as a result). This was a golden era for economic growth, but it had the effect in the UK of concealing significant skills shortages and long-term investment in infrastructure or labour (Glennerster 1995). It is also the case that the post-war period often assumed a world in which there was a single worker (often a man) while women were expected to give up work if they married, an expectation made most explicit in the 'marriage bar' that persisted in some areas of the civil service until the 1970s. Many countries also made use of their colonial histories to employ labour from overseas, but without giving those workers the same citizenship or employment rights. Although there was a lot that appears in retrospect to be good about the post-war economic period, with low unemployment and rising standards of living for many people, others were systematically excluded from those gains (Williams 1989).

From the 1970s onwards, governments regarded full employment – one of Beveridge's 'assumptions' – as less of a priority than achieving low inflation

(Oliver 1996) or of trying to make their economies more competitive (Cerny 1997). This supply-side revolution in thinking (Minford 1991) saw unemployment rates rising, and introduced a complex mix of new regulation and deregulation in the labour market. Regulation was put in place to prevent outright discrimination on the grounds of gender (although this often took decades to enforce), as well as other protected characteristics (such as ethnicity and disability) gradually being incorporated. However, labour markets were also deregulated on the grounds that the labour market needed to become more 'flexible', with employer-based interests often demanding that trades unions take less of a role in their firms, and for greater freedoms to hire and fire staff. The long-term shift from industrial employment to service-based employment has also led, in many countries, to a decline in trade unionism and so a fall in the countervailing forces to employers in labour markets. Negotiations about how labour markets should work have played out in different ways in different countries, some of which met the challenges in consensual ways, but in others there was greater conflict (Thelen 2014). The end result has therefore been more far-reaching in some countries than others, but with the United Kingdom and United States seeing a significant growth in 'platform' jobs, far weaker employment rights, and fewer guarantees about work or pay.

There are several candidates for a 'New Giant' that relates to 'Idleness' in the 2020s. One might be achieving greater vocational education in order to provide skills for the workers of the future, especially as it is likely the labour market is going to be facing even more extraordinary change as smart machines take over an increasing range of jobs. It is not clear, however, how to perform a comparative analysis in these terms, and existing exemplary researchers (Thelen 2014) have explored the history of this subject in admirable detail already.

Instead, the New Giant proposed here is about the quality of work. The labour market has changed so much since the 1970s that, although unemployment remains the headline measure in most reporting of the labour market, the meaning of 'employment' has shifted from predominantly full-time work, often in a single earning household, based on a permanent contract, to something very different by the 2020s (with Hutton 1996 being extraordinarily prescient about these changes thirty years before).

Idleness is often associated with a lack of employment, but because of the changes to the labour market, with a far greater range of possible employment types and durations now available, the unemployment rate alone is no longer a good indicator. Work is important because we need to earn money to live, but also because having meaningful work gives us a role in society that can help us make sense of our lives. Work is not just about providing an income; it can be a crucial contributor to our wellbeing if we regard it as meaningful. Separation from the world of work can deprive us both of the ability to live an independent life, and also of the meaning that work is able to bring. At the same time, having to perform work at very low pay, under high surveillance and with little security, is unlikely to be of benefit to anyone's mental health.

Work is required to pay the bills, but it also needs to be meaningful. Both these elements have increasingly come to present a challenge for large numbers of people since the 1980s with the gradual emergence of a 'precariat' of people in society, living in more or less permanent insecurity (Standing 2014). In such an environment, some groups claiming benefits find themselves labelled as 'scroungers', even as more and more people find themselves claiming them as pay for the poorest groups in society has ceased to rise in line with the rest of it. The New Giant this book considers, then, is about the quality of work and of earnings, as much as it is about unemployment.

The OECD has a range of measures about job quality, but as these measures are not a part of the 'core' range of indicators, data are often incomplete. Within those measures, the earnings quality indicator attempts to capture the extent to which earnings contribute to workers' wellbeing in terms of their average earnings, as well as the distribution of those earnings across the work-force. The measure therefore tries to take into account both earnings quality, and the distribution of those earnings across the workforce (OECD 2014). This gives us a basis for comparing nations in terms of their job quality.

Incorporating Job Quality as the fourth New Giant also fits well with the criteria for inclusion established in Chapter 1. It is conceptually linked to Beveridge's original Giant of Idleness, but recontextualizes it into the 2020s, and the challenges we face now. Job quality is also clearly global in scope – it is not an issue limited to the UK or USA, but the way work and employment relations are changing globally gives us the ability to consider job quality comparatively, and establish which countries appear to be doing best in relation to it, as well as what they are doing. Job quality also reflects a collective action problem – it is about the consequences of our considering ourselves primarily consumers, when we are also workers. By putting our consumer identities first, we call for cheaper prices, faster deliveries, and constant innovation and improvement, but then find ourselves, as workers, having to meet those demands and facing lower pay and less job security. We therefore need to try to work out ways out of the cycle of driving markets through consumer behaviour to find a better balance with our other needs, and to look to countries that appear to be achieving this. Finally, in an age where globalization still dominates our worlds, it is not utopian to be concerned with job quality as it affects most of our lives, and it is an area where some countries seem to be finding a better balance than others. Chapter 7 explores who those countries are, and what we can learn from them.

# NEW GIANT 5: FROM SQUALOR TO ENVIRONMENTAL DEGRADATION

Squalor is a pejorative term that Beveridge used in the context of having been both an academic and (pre-World War 1) an activist in exploring the conditions of the poorest while working at Toynbee Hall at the beginning of the century. He would have seen overcrowding, poor diets and often low levels of sanitation, all of which were facilitating the spread of disease.

There were perhaps three main elements to Squalor in Beveridge's time. The first was housing. People living in overcrowded, damp accommodation without indoor toilets were clearly far more susceptible to health problems. By 1942, bombing of the UK's major cities was a major threat but had not reached the peak (especially in London) that it was to reach later on in the war. Around two million houses were destroyed during World War 2 and one in every six Londoners was affected. Squalor, in terms of housing, was clearly going to be a major challenge.

The second aspect of Squalor falls both inside and outside the home and relates to public health. There had been substantial improvements in public sanitation in the UK in the second half of the nineteenth and early twentieth century, with impetus in London coming from the 'Great Stink' of 1858, and other cities reaching similar conclusions about the importance of building public sewerage systems, despite their financial cost. Within the public health literature there remains a significant debate as to whether improvements in life expectancy in the twentieth century are mostly due to improvements in medicine, or to improvements in public health (Peterson and Lupton 1996). However, it is clear that public health measures, such as the installation of sewerage systems and improved water availability, were an important contributor to improving living conditions, even if, as we saw earlier, it was not until the second half of the twentieth century that indoor toilets became an expected feature of every home.

If the first understanding of Squalor is based on housing, the second area 'zooms out' to include public health issues such as sanitation, and the third moves to another level of abstraction and considers the wider conditions of work and living. The effects of the migration of workers from rural to urban settings, and the conditions under which they lived, were of course a major driver for the critiques of capitalism developed by Marx. With Engels' financial and other support, Marx published *Capital* in 1867, which represented 20 years of the development of his thought. It isn't necessary to be a Marxist to understand the anger that motivated his work, in which he saw those owning the means of production living well, but those actually doing the work existing in dangerous conditions at work, and squalor at home. It also isn't necessary to be a Marxist to understand that the question of the origin of profit is an important one, and links to modern explorations of the balance between those working in productive and extractive areas of economy in society as 'Makers and Takers' (Foroohar 2016) or 'bees and locusts' (Mulgan 2015). A simple summation of this work is that capitalism is an often-unstable alliance of those who create, and those who extract. Both roles have justifications (more obviously for creators), but both also bring challenges.

Despite its appearance as a Giant, Squalor is barely mentioned in the Beveridge Report, but it can be interpreted in terms of emphasizing the importance of housing as well as perhaps the wider public health of community. This led to the government engaging in extensive housebuilding in the years following the war ('homes for heroes', as Bevan put it), even if such building always struggled to meet either public hopes or demand (Lund 2017). As such, Squalor is a mix of factors, bringing together housing, public health, and some of the more adverse consequences of particular forms of capitalism.

Today, housing remains a problem in terms of its cost (especially in large cities), but increasingly also its quality (which relates to some of the less desirable practices that capitalism can foster). Public health, in terms of sanitation and other basic infrastructure, is generally less of a challenge, but clearly emerges in crisis times – such as that of a pandemic, where high-density, low-quality housing areas have often suffered disproportionately from the effects of COVID-19. We still struggle to provide safe environments for people to live in, even though we know more about the link between housing area and life expectancy and a range of social ills (or goods). However, exploring housing environments in particular localities makes larger-scale, cross-national comparisons difficult, and so does not really fit with the macrocomparative analysis that the book is based around. As well as this, there is an even bigger challenge facing us that is conceptually linked to Squalor and which has the potential to be of even greater importance than housing – that of environmental degradation.

From the 1960s onwards there has been an accumulation of evidence that the effects of human behaviour are having adverse consequences on the global environment. In local contexts this link is obvious – if we destroy an area of woodland, it is not available for us or for others, and given the importance of being in and around nature for our wellbeing (Hardman 2020), this is a loss. Historically, where cities have emitted pollution on a large scale, perhaps through large amounts of traffic, or through industrial production generating other forms of pollution, this has harmed the health of those living in those environments. This has led to environmental legislation to limit pollution, as well as measures to try to limit traffic in cities, but it seems that many cities today are struggling to keep within those limits, especially in countries that are trying to develop their economies quickly, but with also richer industrial nations often still seeing rises in pollution levels (Klein 2014).

Looking beyond the local, however, we can also see other linkages. It became clearer in the 1970s that countries were affecting one another's environments, with the most-known example being that of factories in the UK causing pollution clouds that caused acidic rain to fall in Northern Europe. This showed that the consequences of polluting often fall beyond our immediate localities, or even countries. It also became clearer in the 1970s that 'greenhouse gases' often used in products such as aerosols (but not limited to them), were causing damage to the world's ozone layer, and international regulations were put in place to try to limit and reverse the damage. The situation saw some improvement as a result, and demonstrated that collective action in respect of our environment is possible.

However, measures of global temperature in the 1980s and 1990s began to show the emergence of an alarming trend upwards. Perhaps first popularized in former vice-president Gore's film *An Inconvenient Truth*, the issue of global warming, and the possible implications of a rise in global temperatures for the polar icecaps, sea levels, the living conditions of those who would be most immediately affected, and on prevailing weather patterns for almost everyone, began to be clearer.

Since the 1990s, a series of attempts to curb global warming have put in place international agreements, but with key players reluctant to agree or comply with more demanding targets. Innovations such as 'carbon trading' have not really worked in reducing emissions, and concerns continue to grow about the world reaching a point where damage to the environment becomes irreversible (Klein 2014). Extreme weather conditions in countries as far apart as Australia (the bush fires of 2019/20) and the United States (record temperatures in 2021) are increasingly being presented as evidence of climate change.

Despite the accumulation of evidence, and the scientific consensus around global warming, some countries are reluctant to confront it, based primarily around concerns about environmental regulations limiting economic growth. This has created space for especially populist politicians to claim that global warming is not settled science, and to campaign for greater investment in fossil fuels, especially in countries such as the USA and Australia, which still have significant resources to be extracted.

Environmental degradation clearly fits the criteria outlined for being a New Giant. It is conceptually linked to Beveridge's original Giant of Squalor as it has the potential to destroy our living conditions at the most fundamental level. It is truly global in scope, with the actions of individual countries, especially a large presence in industrial processes that pollute, having the potential to cause damage that affects us all. It represents a collective action problem, in that all nations are seeking economic growth, and as individuals we all would prefer to be comfortably affluent, but through our actions as consumers, we are all contributing to environmental problems. Equally, we can also feel power- less in the face of the challenge, feeling no amount of recycling or any number of public transport trips are going to help the global situation.

Finally, despite all the challenges outlined above, it is clear that some coun- tries are making significant progress in terms of meeting their environmental responsibilities and so offer us a path forward. This leads to the matter of identifying what those countries have in common that allow them to alleviate environmental damage.

## CONCLUSION: THE NEW GIANTS

This chapter has presented the New Giants that this book will consider: ine- quality, preventable mortality, the crisis of democracy, poor job quality and environmental degradation. In each case, the New Giant has been explored in relation to the criteria derived from existing research and linked to it. As well as this, it is important that each New Giant can be explored empirically to consider the countries that are most successful in addressing them. This will require a method that can form the basis of such a comparison – and the next chapter turns to the task of working out what would be most appropriate.

## NOTES

1. Figures from https://data.oecd.org/inequality/poverty-rate.htm (accessed on 4 November 2021).
2. Available at https://www.eiu.com/n/democracy-index-2018/ (accessed on 4 November 2021).

# 3.    The method in *Welfare States in the 21st Century*

## INTRODUCTION

Comparing how different countries are dealing with the challenges of the New Giants presents an opportunity to look beyond our own national horizons, to see who appears to be addressing them successfully, and what we can learn as a result. However, it also brings a range of methodological difficulties.

First, there is a limited amount of data available from a limited range of countries. Organizations such as the OECD, the World Bank and the European Union routinely collect and present a range of measures across a number of headings that over the last 50 years or so have become standardized. All countries measure national income, for example, in broadly the same way. However, despite the best efforts of organizations such as the OECD, it is often difficult to construct robust datasets to cover a wider range of factors for a fuller range of countries, and within the measures there are differences in the way that data are collected so that the measures come with numerous notes and adjustments. The data are imperfect.

That the data are imperfect has a number of consequences. First, we have to assume that they contain at least some degree of error, and that means incorporating some degree of leeway in interpretation. Next, it means that, although we would ideally like a phenomenon such as, for example, inequality, to be measured consistently between countries and reflect the same underlying concept, this is never quite going to be the case. There are many measures of inequality, all of which are imperfect, which probably contain errors, and we are left having to do the best we can.

A second point is that country-level measures may or may not be causal in themselves. GDP is the standard measure of national income, and is generally the standard 'control' measure in quantitative, statistical comparative studies (Babones 2013). However, what GDP actually measures is the subject of some considerable debate (Stiglitz, Sen and Fitoussi 2010). GDP appears to be highly correlated with a range of other factors (including levels of pollution, for example), but that doesn't mean GDP causes pollution. It is more likely to be a range of other factors occurring below the national level that are themselves linked to higher levels of GDP, such as the practices countries allow in industrial production and transportation. In that sense GDP is 'epiphenomenal' of other factors occurring at a more micro-level (such as carbon-based industrial development, for example) but does capture at least some of the emergent properties of those lower-level factors. However, some countries with high GDPs are relatively low polluters, and the factors causing pollution may not be necessary for strong economic performance. For each of our country-level measures, we need a credible explanation of why they have been chosen. But that doesn't mean it is not valid to use the higher-level factors – they can be causal (provided we can explain how), even if at least some of their causality occurs at different 'levels' to the country level. Countries do not make decisions or have levels of inequality, but the level of inequality in a country might have significant causal consequences for those living in it.

A third point is that most statistical techniques are based on a range of assumptions that are clearly breached by country-level data. The assumption of independence (or data points being independent of one another) doesn't hold as countries are linked to one another, especially in a globalized era, as never before. Countries are linked in trading blocs, keep a close watch on what other nations are doing, and may have cultural, historical and political links that mean they have a great deal in common. It is also the case that countries tend to have a strong degree of path dependence in most country-level measures. Measures tend to increase or decrease fairly slowly from one year to the next, and although there may be significant change over time, or in the face of a major shock, most country-level measures are very dependent on what has gone before. It makes little sense to assume that Australia in 2015 is very different (or independent) from Australia in 2020.

This non-independence of data means that the 'degrees of freedom' are likely to be over-estimated by standard statistical measures, as the data does not vary as much as those tests would assume. If there are 30 countries in a dataset, but five clear 'clusters' of behaviour within it, with countries in those cluster behaving in remarkably similar ways, then we have far less variation than might first appear.

Putting all of these elements together means that comparative researchers face data where the range of countries that can be examined is limited by the availability of good data, and that the data available are likely to contain errors and be subject to revisions. These data capture important concepts and ideas, but across a more limited range of topics than is ideal, and where we need to be careful is in selecting the most appropriate measures. Data measures are not independent of one another (either by country or by year) and so this limits the extent to which standard statistical tests can provide us with robust comparisons.

# QUALITATIVE COMPARATIVE ANALYSIS (QCA)

QCA is a method created by Ragin (especially 2000, 2008, 2014), and expanded upon by other key authors (see Dusa 2018; Schneider and Wagemann 2012) as a means of systematizing comparative case study work where there are relatively small numbers of cases. It combines a range of ideas to achieve this. First, it assumes that causation is complex rather than linear, so that, rather than looking for the effects of variables independent of one another, it instead looks for patterns of causal factors and how they combine with one another to produce the outcome we are interested in. This is often called 'conjunctional' causation as it looks for conjunctions, or combinations of factors.

QCA is also different from more standard statistical methods in that its solutions are not 'symmetrical' – this means that we need to generate separate solutions for countries that have lower levels of inequality, for example, compared to those that do not, as the two may be very different, and we cannot assume that they exist along a linear function (as they would, for example, in most linear modelling). QCA is also different from standard statistical methods in that its sufficient solution is likely to generate several pathways or causal recipes for the achievement of the outcome under consideration. This is called 'equifinality' and it is the third distinguishing aspect of QCA (alongside causal complexity and asymmetry).

In QCA, data are calibrated, meaning that they are put on a scale rather than the 'raw' data themselves being used. In the earliest forms of QCA, data could take a value of 0 (out of the set) or 1 (fully in the set) only, with 0s reflecting cases for causes that did not have the causal factor or outcome, and 1s where the cause or outcome was present. However, Ragin then (Ragin 2000) updated the method to work with 'fuzzy' sets (technically fsQCA or fuzzy-set QCA), so that data are calibrated onto a scale between zero and one, with zero being entirely out of the set, 1 being fully in the set, and 0.5 the point of indeterminacy, when we can't tell whether the data are in the set or not. So for inequality, if we were calibrating the set of raw data, we might give a 1 to cases where very high levels of inequality exist, 0 to cases where inequality is almost entirely absent (if such cases existed), and then grade other cases between 0 and 1. The process of calibration is complex, but the key thing to bear in mind is that causal factors with outcomes and causal factors that have been deemed to have the cause or outcome will be calibrated with a score between 0.5 and 1, whereas those with the causal factor or outcome absent will have a score between 0 and 0.5 (and are indicated using a '~' character, so ~GINI would be countries without high income inequality.

There are, broadly speaking, three stages to QCA data analysis. The first is the assessment and calculation of 'necessary' conditions. Necessary conditions are those that, if we start with the outcome, are always or nearly always present. In Chapter 4 (inequality) the combination of two factors is found to be both a theoretical and an empirical fit for being necessary amongst the countries without high inequality (~INEQUALITY), that of higher levels of integrative government or higher levels of globalization. To try to keep presentation simpler in the book, I will refer to countries falling in the set of higher-scoring countries as 'higher' and those falling out of that set as 'lower'. Although labelling cases in this way does not always logically follow in QCA, the countries included here are broadly comparable, and this makes the discussion a little easier to follow than describing cases in terms of 'higher' and 'not higher' or 'lower' and 'not lower', depending on the particular causal factor under consideration.

To return to the case of inequality, when either higher levels of integrative government or higher levels of globalization (indicated by the 'or') are present, lower levels of inequality occur most of the time. It is important, however, that this is not simply a statistical relationship and that we can explain why these causal factors might be necessary, which Chapter 4 attempts to do. Finally, it is important that necessary conditions are not simply consistently present but also 'relevant'. What this means is that the causal factors (or combination of causal factors) need to explain a reasonable proportion of the outcome, with around 0.6 (out of 1) being the benchmark used here. This additional criterion is put in place to avoid 'trivial' necessary conditions – those that consistently appear, but have low explanatory power. To give a real-life example, the vast majority of senior roles in large organizations require a person to be a graduate to apply for them, and so being a graduate is a necessary condition. However, it is also probably 'trivial' in that, by itself, being a graduate doesn't explain whether someone gets a senior job or not; there are a range of other factors (once you are a graduate) that are likely to be more important in addition to it.

Once necessary conditions have been established (if there are any), the second stage is the construction of a 'truth table'. Truth tables combine every possible combination of the causal factors (considering whether they are present or not), and assess the consistency of the cases with those causal factors appearing in relation to the outcome we are measuring. The higher the consistency of the causal factors in relation to the outcome, the stronger the case for their being included in the calculation of the sufficient solution (the third stage). Typically, a consistency threshold of 0.8 (out of 1) is used as a starting point. In addition, we might specify other conditions for being included in the solution, most often in this book a reasonable 'PRI' (proportional reduction in inconsistency) score. The reasons for this are a little technical, but it is possible for causal combinations to be present for both an outcome and for the absence of the outcome; and while this is helpful information, it is important that we make a choice of whether a particular causal combination should be included for one or the other. A low PRI score (typically below 0.5 giving a starting point) can give us a clue as to whether we need to look more closely at the case or cases to consider whether they should be included in the solution or not. Cases with low PRI scores are flagged in the relevant chapters and discussed.

The truth tables in this book present the empirical cases only. However, in their full form they also include all possible combinations of causal factors, and so some of these will not exist in reality. These rows are called 'counter-factuals'. For counterfactual rows, QCA makes an assessment, based on the empirical cases, of whether those rows should be included in the calculation of some forms of sufficient solutions. I will not present the counterfactual rows in truth tables in the chapters that follow as doing so makes them very long, and, so in my view, less clear as a result.

The third stage of QCA is the calculation of sufficient solutions. Sufficient solutions are those where, starting from the causal factors, we nearly always find the solution present. Sufficient solutions are important as they give pathways or formulas for the achievement of the outcome we are interested in. With QCA there are likely to be several pathways to the solution (the 'equifinality' discussed above), with each being made up of a mix of factors.

It is standard in QCA to calculate three sufficient solutions. The one presented most prominently is the 'intermediate' one, which includes only the counterfactual rows that confirm with our theoretical expectations (which of course, we have to justify). In addition, counterfactual rows that make no sense (with the combination of 'pregnant' and 'male' being the classic example), including those that are the logical opposite of necessary conditions, are also excluded. What this means is that combinations of causal factors that did not appear in our data will be included in the calculation of the sufficient solution, but only if they match the conditions we theoretically expected to find. This is justified on the basis of offering a way of optimizing the solution, but only with counterfactual rows that match our expectations. In contrast, the 'conservative' solution includes no counterfactual rows at all, and so is based on empirical data only. However, as a result, conservative solutions are often (but not always) more complex as they make less assumptions about the data. Finally, the 'parsimonious' solution includes any non-excluded counter-factual rows that will help simplify the data, whether or not they match our theoretical expectations. In the chapters that follow, all three solutions will be reported, but with the intermediate solution given the most prominence as it is generally regarded as reflecting a balance between rigour (based on analysis of our empirical data) and parsimony (offering the opportunity to achieve some optimization or reduction of the solution, but only for counterfactual rows that conform to our theoretical expectations) (Dusa 2018; Schneider and Wagemann 2012).

The first analysis chapter in the book (Chapter 4, on inequality) will work through this process, explaining each decision and the data as they are presented in full. Chapters after them will include all the data but explain things in a little less depth. I hope, as a result, to be able to show transparency in analytical decisions, but also to help readers who are not familiar with QCA to understand what is going on.

QCA works as a method by itself, but can also be combined with other approaches that explore the data in different ways. This allows a different perspective to be taken on the data, allowing a form of triangulation (if results appear similar) but also a means of considering the data in greater depth where results turn out differently. To that end, the book also includes cluster analysis in its method as a means of exploring the data through a complementary, but different, method.

## CLUSTER ANALYSIS

Cluster analysis is a method based on attempting to find cases that are similar, measured in terms of the 'distance' between the measures included in the analysis. In simple terms, it aims to 'cluster' countries together if they are measured as being close in terms of distance, and to separate those that are measured as being far away.

Adding cluster analysis to the book presents a different perspective on the data, examining the 'raw' data before its QCA calibration, and so can also help in considering the effects of calibration on the data (if any). It is an exploratory method in that it does not aim to demonstrate any kind of causality, but simply to try to see which cases (countries) are most similar or different.

Cluster analysis has become increasingly important in the comparative analysis of health and welfare systems. Bambra's work (Bambra 2007a, 2007b) builds on that of Esping-Andersen (1990) to consider different types of welfare regimes; and most recently, Claus Wendt and his research collaborators (Reibling, Ariaans and Wendt 2019; Wendt 2009) have looked in depth at health systems through a similar lens. It is worth exploring a recent example of Wendt's work because it gives a clear outline of the decisions involved in cluster analysis. Wendt's most recent paper cited above (Reibling et al. 2019), however, is especially important because it makes clear the analytical decisions involved in cluster analysis.

First, the data need to be carefully examined to assess whether they need to be standardized or centred (or both). Cluster analysis generally does both, but if the data series being considered needs different weightings from one another, or if the data are non-continuous then this may not be a good strategy.

Second, we must first consider which distance measure to use. The distance measure looks at the variable in a case and assesses how far, as the name implies, it is from other cases. A range of different measures exist, going from the most basic or 'Euclidian' measure, which assesses the distance in a straight line, and so assumes the presence of continuous data, through to measures such as the 'Manhattan' measure, in which movement between points goes across and up, as it would in a cityscape designed around blocks. Application of the distance measure transforms the data into a 'distance matrix', in which every case is measured in relation to its relevant distance from every other one.

Once we have chosen a distance matrix (or several, if we are comparing the results of different distance measures) we must work out the clusterings, and these can be based upon different algorithms. Clustering can be hierarchical, in which case it can be either agglomerative or disaggregative (depending on whether all cases are assumed to be a separate cluster to start with, and then are gradually combined, the closest first, in each instance, or are assumed to be one cluster that is gradually separated, the farthest apart first), or can be based on a method that aims to find the 'centroids' of clusters by finding and minimizing average (either mean or modal) distances from data points. The advantages of hierarchical clustering are that it allows the clustering to be graphed intuitively through the use of dendrograms, and so makes representing the clusters relatively easy, and that the number of clusters isn't specified in advance – it can be chosen from the dendrogram. However, a great deal in hierarchical clustering depends on the process by which cases are clustered together, which includes and excludes other countries, and this can lead to different results depending on the method of 'linkage' that is chosen. Equally, there will not be a definitive answer as to the 'right' number of clusters from a dendrogram, with several possible solutions often appearing viable. The advantage of k-means and k-modal clustering is that it is run multiple times (the initial cluster 'centroids' are randomly placed) and the best solution taken, meaning that solutions tend to converge on optimal clustering outcomes. The disadvantage is that the number of clusters needs to be specified in advance of the analysis, and clearly influences the clusterings that result, and, as we noted above, hierarchical clustering is often easier to represent because of its use of dendrograms.

Given these complications, it is important to choose linkage methods carefully. In this book, we use Ward and complete clustering. Ward clustering aims to minimize the distance within clusters, and so produce clusterings of cases that are most similar. It is the default method in many statistical packages, including base R (in which the analysis was conducted). Complete clustering, in contrast, assesses potential clusters on the basis of those that are further apart (yet still closest to the potential cluster). While Ward clustering tends to produce tightly packed clusters, complete clustering looks farther afield, seeking to recruit cases that are at the edges of potential clusters. By comparing the results of both methods, we produce different perspectives on the data.

Hierarchical clustering was combined with QCA by Haynes (2017) in what he calls 'Dynamic Pattern Synthesis'. Haynes presents data from a range of different studies exploring over time how hierarchical clustering compares with 'ideal type' QCA, which looks at the combinations of causal factors, but does not include an outcome measure. Haynes's approach, therefore, differs in two key ways from the one used here. First, because Haynes does not use an outcome measure, he is mapping the relationship between a range of factors over multiple time frames. He therefore uses cluster analysis to explore the relationships between variables (and how they cluster) over time, and is using QCA in terms of 'ideal type' set analysis rather than exploring the necessary and sufficient conditions for particular outcomes (in terms of their causal factors) as this book is seeking to do. Haynes is also concerned with how patterns of factors change over time, whereas this book will be concerned with the measured factors and outcomes at a particular point in time. I will not be tracking changes over time because, as noted above, many of the macrocomparative factors I include are strongly path-dependent, and so typically do not change much over time. Haynes's work considers factors at a level of analysis lower than that of the country, and where we might expect to see more variation, making his approach more sensible for his data. Haynes's approach provides key insights for how cluster analysis can aid the understanding of the relationships between cases, and the visual presentation of hierarchical clustering facilitates this. The question, therefore, is how to make use of both causal factors and outcome measures in the analysis in this book.

Similar to Haynes, the results of cluster analysis in this book will be presented in terms of dendrograms. Hierarchical clustering, by being presented in dendrograms, has the advantage of not requiring us to specify in advance how many clusters we think might be in the data, and are therefore a useful exploratory technique. Using hierarchical clustering in this way turns something that is often considered a weakness – its lack of a clear result in terms of the number of clusters present in the data – into a strength because it allows greater flexibility in interpretation, and this is useful when comparing results from another method, QCA.

Conducting cluster analysis in the way the book is attempting raises an additional question. Should the outcome measure used in QCA also be included in the cluster analysis data? As cluster analysis is an exploratory technique, outcome measures (such as inequality) will be effectively treated as just another item of data to measure distances in relation to, rather than differentiating between countries in a more substantial way. Excluding outcome measures means we don't use the full data that are used in QCA, but including them risks countries with very different outcome measures being clustered together if they are similar in their causal factors, and so misrepresenting their performance. In this book the outcome measure or measures will be included, with each chapter explaining how this was accomplished, and how the cluster analysis attempted to balance the need to include as much relevant data as possible, but also to give the cluster analysis a basis for differentiating between countries in terms of the outcome factor as well.

Finally, having examined the data using both cluster analysis and QCA, the results can be compared. This comparison consists of looking at the relationship between the intermediate sufficient solution from QCA, and the two dendrograms produced by the cluster analysis. The aim of this is to see where the two are similar or different, and to gain additional insights about how the countries achieving the outcome (inequality, preventable mortality, etc.) are similar and how they are different.

## PROCEDURE FOR ANALYSIS

Having outlined the book's two main methods, it is now important to explain how they will be used procedurally. Each analysis chapter will begin by producing two hierarchical cluster analyses on the 'raw' data for the area under consideration. Cluster analysis is being used in an exploratory way, and will give us a sense of which countries are most similar, and which most different, based on the range of factors under consideration.

Each chapter will then conduct QCA on the calibrated version of the data, outlining any necessary conditions that were found. Next the truth table for the data will be presented, before moving on to the sufficient conditions, with a special focus on the intermediate sufficient solution for the reasons given earlier. Finding sufficient conditions is the goal of QCA, as they tell us which combinations of conditions appear to consistently lead to the outcome we are concerned with.

Once we have both sets of results, we can compare them. Do countries cluster in similar ways as they are grouped together in QCA sufficient solutions? What similarities and differences are there? Do countries cluster into those that seem to be performing well, and those that are doing less well?

Each chapter from now on will therefore produce perspectives on the data. The cluster analysis will examine the 'raw', uncalibrated data in an exploratory way to see which countries are most similar and most different. The QCA will use calibrated data to attempt to find necessary and sufficient conditions in relation to the outcome. The sufficient solutions can then be compared with those from cluster analysis.

## CONCLUSION

This chapter has explained the book's method, which is a combination of cluster analysis (as an exploratory technique) and qualitative comparative analysis (QCA), used to find both necessary and sufficient conditions for each of the New Giants. Each chapter will then compare the results of these two different forms of analysis to take different perspectives on the data, and to gain as deep an understanding of it as possible.

The next chapter considers the first of the New Giants: inequality.

# 4.  Inequality

## INTRODUCTION

This chapter explores the first of the 'New Giants' – inequality. It considers how a range of possible causal factors combine in countries that achieve lower levels of inequality, looking for the ways in which they are common or different, and finding what 'causal recipes' appear in the qualitative comparative analysis (QCA) as a sufficient solution for them.

The first section provides a summary of the research literature on inequality, considering especially which causal factors will be carried forward into the cluster analysis and QCA. It then moves on to examine the results of the cluster analysis, looking to see the relationships between countries it seems to indicate, before presenting the QCA results. The results of the cluster analysis and QCA solution are then compared. Finally, the conclusion links the findings from the chapter back to the existing research literature, considering what we can learn as a result.

## INTRODUCTION: INEQUALITY IN THE 2020S

In Chapter 2, I made the case that inequality is the first of the 'New Giants', replacing 'Want' from Beveridge's original list. This is not because poverty (its modern equivalent) has disappeared. The meaning of poverty is different now from the 1940s, though, and that brings with it new challenges.

The alleviation of Want was one of the core aims of the proposals in the Beveridge Report, but with a particular definition of 'Want' in mind. Beveridge was seeking to ensure that a 'national minimum' was in place for everyone but set at what he called a 'subsistence' level only. The calculations and tables in the report (Beveridge 1942) linked back to pre-war surveys looking at the cost of 'necessaries' and was mostly based on food, clothing, fuel and light (p.78) (rent represented a more difficult problem because of differences in housing costs). It was also important, as Beveridge required that his scheme would have both flat-rate contributions and benefits, that payments into the scheme would be affordable by everyone in work, and that the overall fund would be separate from general taxation, with contributions to the fund coming from the government, employees and employers, at one third each. These constraints meant that there were definite limits on the benefits that could be offered. The Beveridge scheme was predominantly about providing a subsistence benefit to those whose work had been interrupted, and for those who were of retirement age, with payments into and withdrawals from the scheme being separate from other sources of government income and expenditure. The scheme provided benefits to other 'classes' of the population (with some assumptions about the role of 'Housewives' that have not aged well). It made a clear difference between social insurance (paid for by contributions) and social assistance (for people who had not made the required level of contributions, but which were means-tested and linked to behavioural conditions), as well as making provision for people who suffered from longer-term illness or injury.

As such, Beveridge's conception of alleviating Want was to provide social insurance at subsistence levels to cover interruptions from work, or to give a retirement income, for those who had made the required level of contributions to the scheme. Social assistance was available for other groups, but with conditions attached. The key point here is that the benefits were to be paid at subsistence levels only, with only a limited range of expenditures being taken into account. Beveridge assumed there would be a national health service (to cover sickness) and child benefit payments (to support children), but he did not want his insurance scheme to be over-generous (in case it prevented people from seeking work). Beveridge expected people who wished to receive benefits at rates above subsistence levels (either unemployment or pension) to seek separate provision.

The world, eighty years on, is very different. Beveridge was concerned with what we would now call absolute poverty, the basic resources we need in order to survive. Compared with Beveridge's time, we now earn (on average) far higher incomes. It is hard to make realistic comparisons, but even since the early 1960s most groups have seen their incomes about double in the UK. However, this was from a base where average earners were already earning twice that of the poorest, and the 'P90' (the top 10% of earners) were earning around four times as much. However, the doubling of incomes now means the P90 earn four times as much as the poorest, and the average income has increased by about two and a half times, so that income gaps between those groups have significantly grown. The GINI coefficient (the standard measure of income inequality) has risen from a low of about 0.25 in 1961 up to 0.34 (before housing) or 0.37 (after housing). The largest increase in the GINI measure occurred between 1978 and 1991 (where 51% of the total increase occurred) (Jenkins 2015, p.11), but across the whole period, has risen by about 21% in all.

Over the same period, the percentage of people with an income below a low-income cut-off based on 60% of national income (a standard rate used in the UK and EU) and based on the 2010–11 median has fallen from nearly 70%

in the early 1960s down to around 20% in the 2010s. Absolute poverty has massively declined, but it is still with us. At the same time, the 'gap' between the richest and poorest, as we have seen, has grown.

One possibility is that, as economies grow richer, they become less equal. Looking across the OECD nations (Jenkins 2015, p.12), between the mid-1980s and 2011/12 there is some evidence of this, with the biggest rises in income inequality (amongst the countries included in this book) in the USA, Israel, New Zealand, Germany, and perhaps a little surprisingly, given their social democratic international reputation, Sweden and Finland. However, the increases are uneven, with France, the Netherlands and Belgium seeing almost no change at all, and Greece's GINI coefficient actually falling. Between 1995 and 2013, the GINI coefficient for the EU-15 has remained more or less the same, falling from 31 to 29 in 2001 before gradually rising until 2008, but remaining around the same level (with small fluctuations) since (Jenkins 2015).

## CAUSAL FACTORS

All of the chapters in this book include, as a starting point in exploring causal patterns, two common factors. This allows some consistency in the analysis between the chapters and adds additional depth to the comparison. It is also the case that the two causal factors can be linked to all of the 'New Giants' in a way that is both theoretically and empirically robust.

The first of these two factors aims to capture that achieving social outcomes is necessarily a political act, and the result of a political process. Within research on the structure and form of government, a range of possibilities present themselves as offering a means of classifying the political systems of the different countries included in the book. Perhaps the most widely cited of these are the measures from Lijphart (2012), who classified the democratic processes present in government systems according to what he called the 'executive-parties' and 'federal-unity' dimensions. Lijphart's work is based on a factor analysis of a range of different variables, with the first dimension being based on a range of measures of executive dominance, interest group pluralism and the degree of disproportionality of the electoral system, and the second on measures of the degree of federalism, bicameralism, constitutional rigidity, judicial review and central bank independence. As such, the executive parties measure attempts to capture the extent to which governments are dominated by their executive, or include and incorporate a range of interests. In contrast, the 'federal-unity' measure captures the extent to which the federal government is able to act without blockages or 'veto' points on its decisions.

Whereas there is a reasonable consensus that the first dimension (executive parties) captures an important dimension about the behaviour of government and whether it incorporates a diverse range of interests into policymaking or not (Vis 2007), the second dimension is more controversial because of the wider diversity of measures it includes (Bormann 2010), and so there is a concern as to whether it actually measures federalism or something else. Bearing this in mind, but wanting to incorporate more recent research that includes and addresses some of the critiques of Lijphart's framework, the measure of political systems included in all the chapters in the book comes from Maleki and Hendriks (2016) and they refer to assessing the extent of 'integrative government' versus government that is 'aggregative'. The measure is based on the effective number of parties in the parliament, the number of parties in government, and the total electorate proportionality (which is the combination of whether an electoral system is based on a simple majority or proportional representation, as well as the extent to which presidential elections are proportional). The three numbers are then combined using a geometric mean. Countries such as Switzerland and Israel are scored as being strongly integrative, with Norway, Denmark, Sweden and Finland integrative, but with lower scores. The USA has a low integration (so highly aggregative) score, with the UK also scoring at the low end. This measure has a great deal in common with Lijphart's 'executive parties' dimension, and is strongly correlated to it.

Highly integrative government is included as the first directional expectation causal factor for lower inequality in this chapter. This is because it is important to explore the effects of the structure of political institutions on resulting policy (Peters 2019), and highly integrative government should lead to the inclusion of a wider range of interests in policymaking. A first look at the data suggests that, if we examine the countries graded as having higher levels of integrative democracy, they include a number of countries with a reputation for greater equality. The integrative dimension of democracy therefore gives us some intriguing hypotheses. Are countries with more integrative democratic systems more socially progressive, as a wider range of interest groups will have the opportunity to participate in policymaking? Are those with lower integration therefore less socially progressive, and therefore less likely to be confronting inequality?

The second factor included in all the chapters is tertiary education participation. The inclusion of this factor asks the question as to whether countries with higher levels of tertiary education have made more progress against the New Giants. It has been a centrepiece of much government policy over the last 40 years that higher levels of education should lead to greater economic productivity, but in political terms a more highly educated citizenry also has the potential to make better-informed democratic decisions and foster a more deliberative society (Nussbaum 2010). Governments have actively pursued policies of raising tertiary education participation. Has this approach led to greater engagement in government policymaking with the challenges of the future?

There are three more factors that are included in the specific analysis of inequality in this chapter.

The first is the extent to which globalization has changed the economies and societies of the countries we are considering. Globalization is generally recognized as one of the most important drivers of social change in our time, but it can mean a number of different things in different settings. In some cases, globalization is about financial deregulation and the changing economic environment (Stiglitz 2003) but can also be considered more sociologically in terms of the impact of changing technologies on our sense of identity and self (Giddens 1991a) along with the compression of time and space and the new social risks that this can bring (not least in terms of the environment, our fifth New Giant).

A range of different indexes have been constructed to assess the impact of, and policy change resulting from, globalization on different nations. To try to capture the wide range of concepts involved in globalization, the KOF Globalization Index was chosen[1] for inclusion in the book because of the diversity of relevant measures that are included within it. The KOF index includes a range of measures around the financial aspects of globalization; personal measures around international travel and migration; information-based measures including internet availability, television access and press freedom; and cultural globalization factors including trade in cultural groups and the presence of multinational retailers. Moreover, it considers gender parity and civil liberties, and finally includes political globalization measures including the number of embassies, international NGOs present, and international treaties signed. Like any index, its measures are subject to contestation, but it includes a remarkably wide-ranging list of factors, and has refined its approach over several years. The data included in the book are from the 2019 edition.

Including globalization using the KOF index allows us to consider whether countries rated as more highly globalized are also the most equal – which would portray globalization as more benign – or whether more highly globalized countries also appear to be those with higher levels of inequality.

The next factor included in this chapter attempts to capture the relationship between the global competitiveness of an economy and inequality. Increasing the competitiveness of economies has been a central part of policymaking since the 1980s, with writers of both the left and right stressing the shift in the role of the state in terms of facilitating competition (Cerny 1997; Minford 1991) with Jessop's widely cited typology of changes to the governance of welfare (outlined more fully earlier in the book) suggesting that there has been a shift in the role of government from Keynesianism demand-side management to 'Schumpeterianism' supply-side measures designed to improve competitiveness. Improving competitiveness can come through a range of different strategies, from so-called 'flexicurity' (rising innovation and skill levels) to 'flexploitation' (based on low-cost, low-skill labour) (Viebrock and Clasen 2009). Attempting to capture this diversity is difficult, but in this book we use Global Competitiveness 4.0 index produced by the World Economic Forum.[2] This index comprises a range of measures based around institutions, infrastructure, ICT adoption, macroeconomic stability, health and skills. It therefore has some overlap with the globalization index measure, and the two are correlated at 0.32 with a p value of 0.13, so are not entirely unrelated to one another. However, as will be seen from the sufficient solutions that including both factors generate, the two factors do make different contributions in our understanding, and so add to a better understanding of the causal complexity involved in inequality.

The last factor included in the chapter is that of public social expenditure, measured in terms of US$ (the Purchasing Power Parity measure). Comparing public social expenditure levels should give us an indication of the extent to which governments are committed to either alleviating or correcting what they perceive as occurring in their jurisdictions. We would therefore expect governments more committed to addressing inequality as having higher levels of public social expenditure than those that are not, especially as higher levels of public social expenditure are likely to be the result of higher taxation levels, and therefore based on a more redistributive approach than those with lower levels of public social expenditure. Whilst accepting the excellent work of Hills (2014) and the extent to which social expenditures can income-smooth as well as redistribute, without higher levels of public social expenditure, it is hard to see how significant redistribution to address inequality could occur. It therefore makes sense to assume that higher levels of public social expenditure should be seen in countries with lower levels of inequality.

## INEQUALITY: THE OUTCOME MEASURE

Inequality can be measured in a number of different ways. The most frequently used measure is the GINI coefficient (especially the post-tax and transfers measure), which will also be used in other chapters as a causal factor to achieve some consistency with existing research. However, as inequality is the outcome measure in this chapter, a new factor was created in order to try to capture not only the overall level of inequality (which GINI captures) but also the different effect it has on people living within the countries explored in this book.

The starting point in constructing this factor was the country's post-tax GINI for the most recent available year. However, the post-tax and transfers GINI measure was then combined with the OECD's index in wellbeing inequality to try to capture both income inequality and its possible effects. The OECD measures comprise a range of different variables including the S80/S20 income ratio, the gender wage gap, the extent of long hours in paid work, the gap in life expectancy by education amongst men at age 25, a measure of students with low skills, a measure of the exposure to air pollution, the gender gap in people feeling safe in their countries, the gender gap in hours worked, the share of the population lacking social support, and the share of the population believing they have no say in what the government does. As such, the OECD index attempts to capture both income gaps and a range of possible inequality effects of that gap.

The two measures were correlated (by country) with an r of 0.501, and so a decision needed to be made as to how they might be combined to construct a new factor that maximized the variance explained across the two. To achieve this, a principal components analysis was performed on the data, with the new factor accounting for 0.7507 of the total variance, and with both variables loaded at 0.707 against the first principal component. This new measure, then, seemed fairly robust in achieving a balance between including as many dimensions of inequality as possible, whilst also being comparable between nations.

Having outlined the causal factors and outcome measure used in this chapter, I now move on to the analysis of that data – first through cluster analysis, and then through QCA.

## CLUSTER ANALYSIS

The variables included in the cluster analysis are also those for calculating the QCA solutions in this chapter. They are as follows: (MHINT – the measure of integrative government, Maleki and Hendriks); the extent of measured globalization (based on KOFGLOB19 – the KOF Globalization Index for 2019); their global competitiveness (based on GLOBCOMP19 – the WEF Global Competitive Index 2019); the extent of public social expenditure (PUBSOCEXP – in terms of US$ PPP, from the OECD); and the proportion of the population with tertiary level education (EDUCTERT – OECD measure).

To try to balance the weighting of outcome measures and causal factors, both the OECD and GINI measures of inequality were included separately in the cluster analysis, along with the composite measure that will be used in the QCA section below. This gave the clustering algorithms as much data as possible to differentiate between countries.

As explained in Chapter 3, two clusterings of the data will be presented in each chapter, based on different clustering methods. The clusterings for this chapter have considerable overlap.

Using the Ward.D method the following dendrogram was produced:

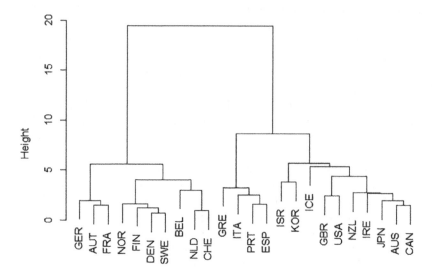

*Figure 4.1      Ward clustering – inequality*

Dendrograms can be read from the top or the bottom. If we read from the top, the first split of countries occurs between predominantly Western European countries on the left, and a more mixed range of countries on the right. The next split then occurs on the right-hand side, further separating broadly southern European countries (GRE, ITA, PRT, ESP) from the rest of the other countries in the cluster, and then ISR and KOR being separated from the others, followed by ICE. After, we see clusters with GBR and the USA close together, along with NZL, IRE, JPN, AUS and CAN all close together.

On the left-hand side, GER, AUT and FRA appear close together, as do NOR, FIN, DEN and SWE, and then finally, NLD and CHE, with BEL as the last country to join the other countries, but closest to NLD and CHE.

The complete linkage clustering method produces a dendrogram that initially appears somewhat different (Figure 4.2), but in fact has considerable overlap with the Ward clustering: it is simply that the countries are ordered on the bottom axis slightly differently.

At the top level (and going from the top of the Figure 4.2 downwards), the first split in the clustering path is a little different from that of the Ward clustering with Iceland, New Zealand, Ireland, Australia and Canada appearing with the West European countries rather than on the right-hand side of the diagram, albeit on the first 'fork' of the left-hand cluster, so being separable from them. Beyond that, things are very similar, with clusterings (on the right-hand side) of Portugal and Spain, then Italy and Greece, with the United Kingdom

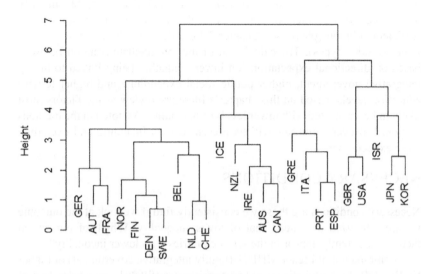

*Figure 4.2    Complete clustering – inequality*

(which always appears as GBR in international datasets) and the USA close together. However, Japan is positioned closer to South Korea and Israel than in complete clustering, whereas in Ward.D it is closer to Australia and Canada. The left-hand side of the clustering (as it appears in the dendrogram above), comprising the group on the left starting with Germany, Austria and France, is almost identical to the Ward.D clustering, however.

The cluster analysis, then, gives us a preliminary sense of how countries lie in relation to one another in respect of the data. A next step, were we conducting cluster analysis alone, would be to examine the data and try to work out what similarly clustered countries have in common, as well as to try to work out how many clusters of countries the data suggests. Rather than do that next, however, we will now move on to QCA as a means of exploring the data in this chapter through a different lens, as well as considering especially in terms of the results of the analysis of sufficiency. QCA adds to cluster analysis by considering the outcome factors in relation to the outcome, rather than including all as data on a similar basis.

## QUALITATIVE COMPARATIVE ANALYSIS (QCA)

QCA considers how causal factors combine in different patterns in relation to the outcome measure. For QCA we must also set 'directional expectations', which are the initial theoretical assessment of the factors that are most likely to be present in the solution, based on existing research (having some similarity to hypotheses) and which form the basis of the calculation of the intermediate sufficient solution (please see Chapter 3 for a detailed discussion of the different solution types). The calculation of the intermediate solution below is based on directional expectations on lower inequality being linked to highly integrative government, higher public social expenditure and higher tertiary education levels, based on this chapter's literature review as the factors most likely to be associated with lower levels of inequality. As noted in the methods section, however, solutions will be presented both including and excluding these expectations.

## NECESSARY CONDITIONS

Necessary conditions are those we consistently find if we look at the outcome we are interested in – here, that of lower inequality. Which of our causal factors consistently appear in the set of countries with lower inequality?

A combination of higher MHINT (highly integrative government) or higher KOFGLOB (high globalization) had consistency of 0.901 and a relevance of 0.623. This makes this combination of factors worth our attention, but in order to be included as necessary they must have both empirical support and a strong theoretical fit. Empirically, we need measures that are highly consistent (at or around 0.9, effectively 90%). However, results must also have reasonable relevance scores. An irrelevant necessary condition is one that is always present in an outcome but has no causal link and does not vary with it. It is necessary for lower inequality to first have oxygen present, but having oxygen present tells us nothing useful about lower inequality (at least on Earth). The relevance measure explores not only whether a causal condition is present (which is captured by consistency), but also whether it appears to vary in line with the outcome. This produces the 'relevance' (or to give its full name, 'relevance of necessity') measure. Ideally, we are looking for scores of at least 0.6.

As well as empirical measures, the factors we wish to include as necessary must also be supported theoretically or through previous empirical research. There are good theoretical reasons for expecting that a highly integrative government would lead to lower inequality as that type of governance is more likely to incorporate more interests into the decision-making process, so may have a tendency to try to govern for a wider cross-section of people than governments that do not include as wide a range of interests. Higher globalization, in contrast (higher KOFGLOB), is not as obvious a candidate for lower levels of inequality. However, higher globalization could have an effect on reducing inequality as well as increasing it, and advocates of free trade would probably strongly argue in favour of the former (Legrain 2004).

As such, the combination of either highly integrative government, or higher globalization, appears to be necessary for lower inequality. This necessary condition is carried forward as a means of considering 'remainder' or 'counter-factual' rows in the data (which will be explained below), and we would also expect to see one or other (because they are joined by a logical 'or') of these terms in our sufficient solutions.

The next stage of analysis, however, is to construct a 'truth table'. The truth table lists the causal factors, and identifies each case in relation to them. It then locates each case in terms of its combination of causal factors, and assesses the extent to which that combination is consistent with the outcome factor – here that of lower inequality. The truth table can be seen in Table 4.1.

Understanding a truth table requires us to look at each row of the data carefully. The first row here contains countries that score in the low range in fuzzy-set terms for each causal factor, so have fuzzy-set scores across the board between 0 and 0.5. These scores then act as a means of categorizing the countries for the next stage of analysis, as it can be demonstrated that each country has one, and only one, combination of causal factors that best fits its calibrated data profile (Ragin 2008). In the first row, the combination of low scores across all of the causal factors categorises the cases of Greece and New Zealand, and is not consistent with lower inequality (with a consistency score of 0.682). The generally accepted consistency threshold to initially consider the truth table is 0.8 (effectively 80%) for inclusion in the sufficient solution (setting 'OUT' in the truth table to 1). However, we must also consider the 'PRI' score (which stands for proportional reduction in inconsistency) as some row profiles can be consistent with both the outcome and the negation of the outcome (here, with both lower and higher inequality). We therefore need to examine the PRI scores of high consistency countries to make sure we include them in one solution only - it makes no sense to include them in both the solution for both lower and higher inequality. A PRI score of at least 0.55 (along with a high consistency score) would suggest that this is less likely to be a problem, but where the PRI score falls below that, a conscious decision needs to be made as to whether the country should be included or not.

This truth table has only a couple of rows that require care and additional interpretation. The USA, Spain, Canada and the UK are on rows that are below the 0.8 consistency threshold, but quite close to it (with consistency scores of 0.771, 0.776 and 0.786, for both Canada and the UK, respectively), but they also have low proportional reduction in inconsistency (PRI) scores, suggesting their pattern of causal factors might fit better with higher inequality instead.

Italy has a consistency of 0.832, so above the consistency threshold, but with again a low (0.419) PRI score, so is treated here as a higher-inequality country instead through the use of a PRI threshold of 0.5 to avoid cases appearing in both the higher and lower inequality solutions.

*Table 4.1*    *Inequality truth table*

| MHINT | KOFGLOB | GLOBCOMP | PUBSOCEXP | EDUCTERT | OUT | CONSIST | PRI | CASES |
|---|---|---|---|---|---|---|---|---|
| 0 | 0 | 0 | 0 | 0 | 0 | 0.682 | 0.193 | GRE, NZL |
| 0 | 0 | 1 | 0 | 1 | 0 | 0.649 | 0.164 | AUS, JPN, KOR |
| 0 | 0 | 1 | 1 | 1 | 0 | 0.771 | 0.332 | USA |
| 0 | 1 | 0 | 0 | 0 | 0 | 0.650 | 0.005 | PRT |
| 0 | 1 | 0 | 0 | 1 | 0 | 0.776 | 0.129 | ESP |
| 0 | 1 | 0 | 1 | 1 | 1 | 0.970 | 0.875 | IRE |
| 0 | 1 | 1 | 0 | 1 | 0 | 0.786 | 0.276 | CAN, GBR |
| 0 | 1 | 1 | 1 | 1 | 1 | 0.850 | 0.565 | FRA |
| 1 | 0 | 0 | 0 | 1 | 1 | 0.839 | 0.568 | ICE, ISR |
| 1 | 0 | 0 | 1 | 0 | 0 | 0.832 | 0.419 | ITA |
| 1 | 1 | 0 | 1 | 0 | 1 | 0.904 | 0.643 | AUT |
| 1 | 1 | 0 | 1 | 1 | 1 | 1.000 | 0.999 | BEL |
| 1 | 1 | 1 | 0 | 1 | 1 | 0.999 | 0.996 | NLD |
| 1 | 1 | 1 | 1 | 1 | 1 | 0.990 | 0.970 | FIN, GER |
| 1 | 1 | 1 | 1 | 1 | 1 | 1.000 | 1.000 | DEN, NOR, SWE, CHE |

The truth table (Table 4.1) presents the calibrated empirical data for this chapter. However, QCA can also examine combinations of factors that did not occur empirically, and incorporate them into its calculations of sufficient solutions. As the world does not come with all of our analytical categories fully occupied, it has what is called 'limited diversity' in which every possible combination of causal factors is unlikely to occur. Sometimes combinations will be impossible, but in other situations they are possible but simply haven't happened. These 'counterfactual' or 'remainder' rows can be included as a means of simplifying solutions, in which case they can be assumed to be consistent, or inconsistent with the outcome, depending on whether that combination of factors would lead to a more concise solution. We remove any counterfactual rows that are logically impossible. If conditions are necessary, their opposite cannot be included in sufficient solutions, and other combinations may also be self-contradictory, so need to be removed. After that, there are three options.

First, we can include only counterfactual rows that fit with previous theoretical or empirical work. In specifying our 'directional expectations' above, what we were doing was making clear which counterfactual rows are available to calculate the sufficient solution. These assumptions, however, make no difference in relation to empirical data, but do apply when considering whether counterfactual rows should be included. Here, if counterfactual rows help simplify the solution, and fit with directional expectations, they are also included in the calculation of the intermediate sufficient solution. This approach is generally held to offer a sensible compromise, and so this solution, the 'intermediate' one, will form the primary basis of reporting below.

Second, we can exclude all counterfactual rows and calculate sufficient solutions based on empirical data only. This approach makes the fewest assumptions, but also presents the most complex solutions. This is the 'conservative' solution, which will be reported after the intermediate solution in each chapter.

Third, we can include all remaining counterfactual rows in the calculation of the solution. Taking this approach leads to what is called the 'parsimonious' solution, as it is likely to be the simplest. As with the conservative solution, it will be reported after the main presentation of the intermediate solution, but not given as much prominence.

## SUFFICIENT SOLUTION

The intermediate sufficient solution, as noted above, was produced with directional expectations of highly integrative government, higher public social expenditure and higher tertiary education. It contained three solution pathways, and was as follows:

*Table 4.2        Intermediate sufficient solution – inequality*

| Solution | Consistency | PRI | Coverage | Unique Cov. | Cases |
|---|---|---|---|---|---|
| MHINT* KOFGLOB *PUBSOCEXP | 0.929 | 0.876 | 0.583 | 0.127 | AUT, BEL, FIN, GER, DEN, NOR, SWE, CHE |
| KOFGLOB* PUBSOCEXP *EDUCTERT | 0.906 | 0.823 | 0.563 | 0.107 | IRE, FRA, BEL, DEN, NOR, SWE, CHE |
| MHINT* KOFGLOB *GLOBCOMP *EDUCTERT | 0.984 | 0.972 | 0.477 | 0.054 | NLD, DEN, NOR, SWE, CHE |
| MHINT *~KOFGLOB *~GLOBCOMP *~PUBSOCEXP *EDUCTERT | 0.839 | 0.568 | 0.208 | 0.062 | ICE, ISR |

The sufficient solution here has four pathways, and has an overall consistency of 0.844, and a coverage of 0.810. This means it is consistent at a level of 0.844 (so we might expect some cases that don't fit entirely with it), and its coverage of all the countries with lower inequality is 0.810 (again, out of 1), and so, although it has high coverage, some of the countries with lower inequality have other combinations of factors. We will discuss below cases that have the combination of causal factors in the sufficient solution, but which don't have lower inequality (and so are 'deviant for consistency') and those that have lower inequality, but do not have the causal factors in the sufficient solution (and so are 'deviant for coverage').

The first solution pathway combines highly integrative government with higher globalization and higher public social expenditure, and covers the cases of Austria, Belgium, Finland, Germany, Denmark, Norway, Sweden and Switzerland. There are no cases deviant for consistency in this solution pathway (so all the cases with this combination of causal factors have lower inequality). This pathway has a consistency of 0.929 and the highest coverage and unique coverage of the pathways (0.583 and 0.127), suggesting it is empirically an important solution. Unique coverage, as the name implies, is that part of the outcome which is accounted for by this combination of causal factors, and does not overlap with other pathway solutions. In QCA, pathway solutions can overlap where they have causal conditions are in common. This solution pathway also includes both of the solution terms identified earlier as 'necessary' (MHINT and KOFGLOB).

The second solution pathway combines higher globalization, higher public social expenditure and higher tertiary education. It covers Ireland, France, Belgium, Denmark, Norway, Sweden and Switzerland, so overlaps in terms of case coverage with the first solution pathway for Belgium, Denmark, Norway, Sweden and Switzerland. This means that, although the solution has coverage of 0.563, it has lower unique coverage than the first pathway (0.107). It also contains no cases deviant for consistency, and adds to our theoretical knowledge as it substitutes highly integrative government (first pathway) for higher tertiary education, and so overlaps with the first solution pathway while not entirely duplicating it, bringing new countries into the solution term. This pathway includes 'KOFGLOB' as the necessary condition from earlier analysis.

The third solution pathway has four causal conditions, and extends the coverage of the sufficient solution to include the Netherlands (but has Denmark, Norway, Sweden and Switzerland in common with the first two solution pathways). It combines causal factors from the first two solution pathways, including both the necessary conditions from pathway one. Again, it has no cases deviant for consistency.

Finally, the fourth solution pathway is the most complex, and brings in Iceland and Israel into the sufficient solution, but with Israel as a case deviant for consistency. This pathway, in common with the third pathway, has low unique coverage because of the overlap of causal factors with other pathways. It includes MHINT from the necessary solution, but also has ~KOFGLOB, lower levels of globalization, which means that this part of the solution is the inverse of pathways one and three. However, the necessary condition is still met as it requires either MHINT or KOFGLOB to be included – and that is the case here.

The conservative solution is identical to the intermediate solution, so that the inclusion of directional expectations did nothing to simplify the intermediate sufficient solution. The parsimonious solution simplifies the four-pathway solution to two pathways only (which is perhaps unsurprising given how much the causal factors overlap in the first three solution pathways) and is simply MHINT*~PUBSOC (for Iceland, Israel and the Netherlands) and KOFGLOB*PUBSOC (for all the others).

As outlined above, the sufficient solution for lower inequality has one deviant case for consistency (Israel, in pathway four), and one case deviant for coverage (Canada). If we present a plot of the solution against the set membership of the countries with lower inequality, we can see Israel appears some distance from the other countries, making clear its status as something of an outlier in the solution. Looking back to our truth table, Israel appears on the same row as Iceland, with Iceland having lower levels of inequality, but not Israel. This difference in outcome gives us a clue as to how we can carry out further, more detailed comparative analysis.

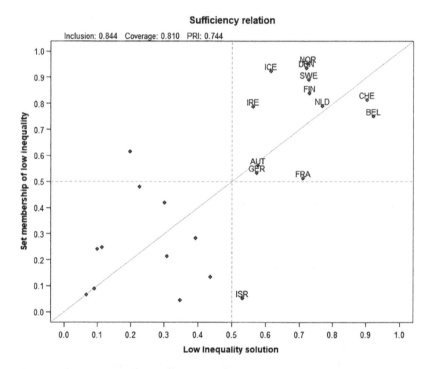

*Figure 4.3      Inequality sufficiency relation*

## COMPARISON OF CLUSTER ANALYSIS AND QCA

We are now in a position to compare the cluster analysis and QCA solutions. In terms of the QCA solutions, the first solution pathway included Austria, Belgium, Finland, Germany, Denmark, Norway and Switzerland. All of these countries are on the left-hand side of both the Ward.D and complete linkage dendrograms (with France and the Netherlands, which are on the left-hand side of the clustering missing from the solution, but present in the second and third solution pathways, respectively).

The second solution pathway in the QCA covered the cases of Ireland, France, Belgium, Denmark, Norway, Sweden and Switzerland. All but one of these countries (IRE is the exception) are again on the left-hand side of both the Ward.D and complete linkage dendrograms. This highlights Ireland as being a case that is worthy of further consideration as to how it is different to the other countries in those solution pathways.

The third solution pathway covered the Netherlands, Denmark, Norway, Sweden and Switzerland. As the third solution pathway was in many ways a combination of the first two pathways, it isn't surprising to find that all these countries are on the left-hand side of both the Ward.D and complete linkage dendrograms.

Finally, the fourth QCA solution pathway included Iceland and Israel, both of which are on the right of both Ward.D and complete dendrograms, but in that pathway Israel was deviant for consistency. Iceland, then, is alone in the solution as appearing on the right-hand side of clustering, and so worth additional exploration. It is worth noting, however, that Iceland appears as a country that is not closely clustered to others in the Ward.D or complete linkage dendrograms. If we read the two dendrograms from top to bottom, Iceland is the first to separate itself from the rest of the countries in each case, and so would seem to have the least relationship with other countries. In other words, Iceland appears as an outlier in terms of this data.

Finally, Canada was the case in our QCA sufficient solution, which was deviant for coverage, and so it is important that we consider it again. Canada is interesting in that it is clustered tightly with Australia in both dendrograms, whereas Australia is categorized in the QCA truth table with Japan and Korea instead (with Canada on the same truth table row as the UK). Canada, then, appears to have a series of causal factors that are more ambiguous than several other nations, and achieves its lower inequality perhaps despite, rather than because of them. Given this, it is hard to recommend that the pattern of causal factors in Canada is a strong causal recipe for others to follow.

Overall, the countries on the left side of the dendrograms appear to have considerable explanatory fit with those achieving lower inequality as an outcome. The two sets of results therefore complement one another at the top level, suggesting a strong degree of triangulation there. At the same time, the comparison of the cluster analysis and the QCA results has helped to identify more cases – especially Ireland – that had not been suggested by either set of results as requiring further investigation, but where there is clearly a case for looking deeper.

The next section examines the results in more detail, looking to see what we can learn from them, and considers the countries identified as being especially important in the results in greater detail.

## DISCUSSION

The most significant QCA sufficient solution pathway (in terms of country coverage) was a combination of highly integrative government, higher globalization (so including both the necessary conditions) and higher public expenditure. This seems to suggest that countries with highly integrative government (which is present in three of the four solution pathways), and which include a range of different interests and views, might be more successful in confronting inequality than those that are based on political systems less likely to be as inclusive. Highly integrative government, in conjunction with the other factors in three of the solution pathways, therefore appears at the root of solution pathways for lower inequality.

Higher public social expenditure appears in two of the four solution pathways. It also makes theoretical sense for higher levels of public social expenditure to be linked, along with other causal factors, as being present in lower inequality countries. Countries that engage in higher levels of public social expenditure are likely to be redistributing resources at higher levels than those that do not, acting as both a brake on inequality, and as a means of ensuring minimum standards for the poorest.

The presence of the third factor in the first solution term – higher levels of globalization – is at first glance perhaps more surprising. However, it is important to remember that QCA presents solutions where factors are combined – in the first solution pathway, higher globalization is combined with highly integrative governmental systems and higher levels of social expenditure, and in the second solution pathway with higher levels of tertiary education and higher public social expenditure – so these factors cannot be considered as working independently of one another as they would be in many forms of standard multivariate analysis.

The first solution pathway, although it has the highest coverage and unique cover, is not the only route to lower levels of inequality. A key part of QCA is 'equifinality', in which there can be more than one solution pathway, and the pathways can overlap in terms of their causal factors. This is clearly apparent in the second solution pathway, which includes five of the countries present in the first, but adds Ireland and France. This means the causal factors are slightly different to reflect the different countries included. Once again, we have higher public social expenditure and higher levels of globalization, but here they combine with higher levels of tertiary education. This pathway suggests that any negative consequences from higher levels of globalization can be ameliorated by higher levels of tertiary education and higher public social expenditure in a similar way to the combination of higher levels of integrative government and higher public social expenditure in the first solution pathway. This solution is again theoretically coherent: countries that are aiming for a high skill workforce (the 'flexicurity' model) may be successful in a more globalized economy so long as there is investment in that education, as well as in public social expenditure more generally.

The addition of the second solution pathway shows a different but complementary lens on the patterns of causal factors for lower inequality, but there are countries – Belgium, Denmark, Norway, Sweden and Switzerland – that have the causal factors which the first and second pathways share. Four of those countries, along with the Netherlands, make up the third solution pathway, which includes higher integrative government, higher levels of tertiary education and higher levels of globalization than the first two pathways, but adds a higher score on the global competitiveness index as well. This pathway has the highest consistency of all the solution terms (0.984), and suggests that being both highly global in outlook, as well as aiming to be internationally competitive, can still produce lower inequality, provided that this is combined with integrative government and higher levels of tertiary education – a highly skilled workforce. This pathway again re-emphasizes the importance of the 'flexicurity' approach to considering the changes to the global economy since the 1980s; provided there is state investment, especially in education, and that government incorporates a range of interests, it is possible for globalization to take a different pathway to countries that have instead aimed to be competitive through a low skill, low employment rights route ('flexploitation') instead.

The fourth QCA sufficient solution pathway is the most complex of the four, while at the same time covering the least countries. The fourth pathway solution has lower global competitiveness, lower globalization and lower public social expenditure. However, it contains two countries only, and one of those is deviant for consistency (Israel). As such, although the combination of factors in the fourth pathway is interesting, it is a less typical solution, and so needs to be interpreted in that light.

## CASES FOR FURTHER INVESTIGATION

The first two cases highlighted as needing further investigation were those of Israel and Iceland. Israel is deviant for consistency, so appears in the QCA sufficient solution when that country does not have lower inequality. Israel appears on the same truth table row as Iceland, and the causal factors they share, as noted above, are unusual in the solution. While Iceland has lower inequality, Israel does not. How much of a problem is that for the solutions presented here?

The key point here is that, to paraphrase much wiser writers that have come before, all models are wrong, but some are useful. Both QCA and cluster analysis are abstractions – they are methods that try to isolate some key factors and build a model around them. They cannot capture all the causal complexity that exists in the world, or account for every possible contingency. Both Iceland and Israel are interesting and important cases, but they are also different both culturally and historically from most of the other countries here. They represent cases from which we can learn (and it is indeed interesting that they share the same pattern of causal factors, despite being so different in many other aspects), but the majority of the learning in this chapter is really concerned with the patterns of causal factors in the other three pathway solutions. They consistently point to a range of factors that, in combination, appear to produce lower inequality with a very high degree of consistency, and where we can also present a clear explanation for why those factors, in combination, should lead to that outcome.

If Israel and Iceland are unusual in terms of their presence in the QCA solution, then Canada is important as it is missing from it. Canada has lower inequality, but it does not have any of the causal pathways or recipes that appear in the solution.

Canada has the same pattern of causal factors as the United Kingdom, having lower integrative government, higher globalization, higher global competitiveness, lower social expenditure, and higher tertiary education. Both countries therefore have some of the terms present in different solution pathways (especially higher globalization and higher tertiary education), but they lack either highly integrative government or higher social expenditure. In terms of its governance model, Canada is actually closer to Germany than to the USA, and its fuzzy set score puts it as the very last country in the 'low' integrative government set. However, a boundary has to be drawn somewhere in the calibration process, and Canada falls just, and only just, into the lower set for integrative government. Without that difference to the other countries in the lower inequality solution, Canada would be a stronger fit. This provides us with a reasonable explanation of why Canada achieves lower inequality despite its lower score for integrative government – it is because it is measured as only just falling into the set of countries with that feature.

The last country we need to look at again is Ireland. This country appears in the solution term for lower inequality but is 'on the wrong side' of the cluster analysis, appearing separately from the other countries achieving lower inequality. What is happening there?

In the Ward clustering, Ireland appears nearest to New Zealand and Japan on the right-hand side of the dendrogram, whereas for complete clustering it is nearest to New Zealand (again) but also Australia and Canada. Ireland is alone on its QCA truth table row with a pattern of ~MHINT*KOFGLOB*GLOBCOMP*PUBSOC*EDUCTERT. Ireland, then, scores highly across all of the causal factors generally present in countries achieving lower inequality, except in its score for integrative government. The cluster analysis appears to be locating Ireland in the dendrogram based upon this lack of integrative government, without which Ireland is closer to Finland and Germany in terms of its pattern of causal factors. As such, the clustering algorithm appears to be making a difference here, which is overemphasizing that factor as differentiating between cases, and which works well in identifying differences between cases for the most part, except for Ireland.

In all, then, we can reasonably account for both the solutions from QCA and cluster analysis, and see which factors, in combination, appear across the countries in the sample set, to be linked to lower inequality. The next section presents the chapter's conclusions in terms of inequality as a New Giant.

## CONCLUSION

This chapter considered inequality, the first of the New Giants. It explored inequality in the context of combinations of different factors that allow international comparisons to be made – the extent of integrative government and tertiary education, the degree of globalization and international competitiveness, and the level of social expenditure. These factors were measured in relation to an index made up of the post-tax GINI coefficient and the OECD's index of wellbeing inequality.

Cluster analysis gave an initial sense of the data, with dendrograms producing a split between a number of countries in Western Europe (on the left-hand side) and a mix of other nations on the right. Within those two broad clusters, other links could be seen (between Germany, France and Austria, for example), but, at the highest level, there seemed to be a divide based on nine or ten Western European countries and the rest of the sample – all of which have lower levels of inequality.

The QCA results have a strong overlap with those from the cluster analysis, with the countries on the left of the dendrograms featuring strongly in sufficient solutions. The sufficient solutions were based on necessary conditions of either highly integrative government or higher globalization, with the former also forming part of the directional expectation for the calculation of the intermediate sufficient solution.

QCA sufficient solutions give us combinations of factors that appear in lower inequality countries, with key factors having considerable overlap, especially in the first three solution pathways that include the majority of the countries in the solution. Highly integrative government appears in two of the three main solution pathways (as well as being in the fourth), with higher public social expenditure, higher tertiary education and higher globalization also appearing in two of the three main solution pathways. These factors, then, in different combinations (but which are all present for Denmark, Norway, Sweden and Switzerland) appear to be crucially related to lower inequality.

We can also suggest why these factors might be important for lower inequality. Highly integrative government may mean governments need to work more inclusively, taking into account more interests and avoiding to a greater extent marginalized groups being excluded from both economy and society.

Higher public social expenditure is likely to mean countries are more committed to redistributionary policies. Higher tertiary education levels should mean a country has a higher skill base, and so more people having access to better jobs. A highly globalized economy is not necessarily regarded as a factor that might be linked to lower inequality in existing work, but in the context of being in combination with other factors, what appears to be the case here is that, in countries such as Denmark, Norway, Sweden and Switzerland, lower inequality and higher globalization can exist at the same time provided combinations of other factors, such as having two of higher integrative government, higher public social expenditure, or higher tertiary education, but for these particular countries, all three.

As such, the solutions from this chapter appear to justify using QCA as the book's main method, with their emphasizing the importance of considering causal factors in different combinations rather than one at a time. Equally, the existence of Iceland, with its very different causal recipe, also shows the importance of equifinality.

A number of countries were highlighted in the analysis as being important, as not every country fits within the QCA sufficient solution. Iceland offers a very different route to lower inequality than other countries, but it is perhaps less a template for others to follow because of its rather unique history. Israel has a similar combination of causal factors as Iceland, but it does not achieve lower inequality, again perhaps highlighting that Iceland is unusual in its achievement of lower inequality, and is clearly a country that is worth exploring in greater depth. Canada falls outside the QCA sufficient solution because its calibrated integrative government score falls just outside the 'higher' range, but other than that fits the solution, and is therefore only just a deviant case. It is important to emphasize that a limited range of causal factors can never capture the full complexity of the world, even if the solutions here seem to do remarkably well in providing a range of causal recipes that work in capturing the countries with lower inequality in the sample.

Having considered inequality, the book now moves on to the next of the New Giants, preventable mortality. As explained in this chapter, two of the causal factors included here – integrative government and tertiary education – will be included in the analysis for all the New Giants, both because they are credible as causal factors and because they allow comparison between the chapters.

## NOTES

1.  Available at https://kof.ethz.ch/en/forecasts-and-indicators/indicators/kof-glob alisation-index.html (accessed on 8 November 2021).
2.  Available at http://reports.weforum.org/ (accessed on 8 November 2021).

# 5.   Preventable mortality

## INTRODUCTION

Chapter 2 made the case that preventable mortality should be the New Giant replacing disease from Beveridge's original list. As I explained there, medical practice has been transformed over the last 80 years, as has our understanding of the importance of social conditions in relation to health and wellbeing, and there is now much wider acknowledgement of mental as well as physical health. Although we still face huge challenges in fully understanding and treating complex, multi-faceted diseases such as cancer, and conditions such as arthritis and dementia blight so many lives, medical understanding has come an incredible distance from the 1940s, with a range of treatments now possible that would have been unimaginable then. However, despite these improvements in our understanding of health and wellbeing, we are now seeing rises in what have been called 'deaths of despair' (Case and Deaton 2020) and it remains the case that, even in developed nations, not everyone has access to the medical treatments that they need. Our knowledge of health and healthcare is extraordinary compared with that of the 1940s, but that improvement in knowledge, and the range of treatments it has brought, does not benefit everyone equally.

An extreme example of how far medical practice has come is a favourite story of Gawande, who presents it in his book *The Checklist Manifesto* (Gawande 2010) as well as in his Reith Lectures. Gawande outlines a case from the *Annals of Thoracic Surgery* concerning a three-year-old girl, who, when out for a walk with her parents in a small Austrian town, fell through the ice of a pond. It took 30 minutes before her parents were able to get her body from the bottom of the pond, and a further eight minutes for an emergency team to arrive. That team found the little girl unresponsive, but they continued with the cardiopulmonary resuscitation her parents had begun. She was taken to a hospital that went through a series of processes of incredible complexity, gradually bringing the little girl back to life over a period of two days. Several years on, she appears to have suffered no significant long-term consequences. The point Gawande is making is of the miraculous capability of medicine, but also that the little girl's miraculous recovery is not normal (or it wouldn't be in a case report). Most people who fall through the ice in ponds and who are under the water for any length of time do not survive. Instead, Gawande is demonstrating modern medicine's extraordinary complexity, the incredible things it can achieve when harnessed in a concerted way, but the potential of things to go wrong because of that complexity. Penicillin, Gawande suggests, has given us a false impression that we can be simply cured of almost any disease. The antibiotic revolution routinely cures us of conditions that were life-threatening to those experiencing them in the nineteenth and even first half of the twentieth century. However, the widespread use of antibiotics has also led to the dangers of 'resistance' to them, and the threat that the drugs could become obsolete. Medicine is hugely complicated, and when we combine that complexity with the importance of the social factors outlined in Chapter 2 (and below), along with health systems often struggling to provide access for all their people, then the delivery of effective healthcare becomes a huge challenge. The two problems this suggests are, first, less about what medicine 'knows' through its research, trials and experience, as an abstract collective body of knowledge, but instead about how that knowledge can be accessed on a population level. Second, there are deep questions, especially prevalent during the pandemic in which this book is being written, about the relationship between medical knowledge and political life, and the extent to which medical understanding should drive political decisions so that as many people as possible are able to live healthy and long lives despite the social conditions they may find themselves in.

This chapter attempts to explore how successful (or otherwise) different countries are in organizing their societies to look after the health and wellbeing of their people. It begins by explaining and justifying the causal factors it will include in its analysis, along with how the outcome measure was derived.

## CAUSAL FACTORS

This chapter's focus on preventable mortality attempts to capture the differences between countries in relation to a range of factors, including the health system, in supporting the health and wellbeing of the people who live within them. The challenge of considering which factors are relevant for exploring preventable mortality is that such a wide range of factors can potentially be relevant. Advocates of what has become known as the 'social determinants of health' (Marmot 2015; Marmot and Wilkinson 2005) show links between our health and a range of social factors, especially inequality. Inequality, however, can be measured in a number of different ways, and overlaps and intersects with a range of other factors, including poverty levels, the differential experience of classes and groups in society (especially those from minority and marginalized groups), but also the quality of housing, food and work. Health, in this view, is very much a factor of the position people hold in society, but in the aggregate, it is often the distribution of these factors that has the strongest health effects. Poorer health is therefore seen as a function of inequalities in these other factors; it is socially determined.

Looking at a range of measures over the last two decades, the OECD (2017b) found links between gains in life expectancy (not quite what this chapter is measuring, but certainly relevant to it), and suggest the biggest contributory factors were increases in health spending, increases in education levels, and rising national income, along with falling smoking and alcohol consumption. All these factors make theoretical as well as empirical sense – increased spending on healthcare, where it is making services more accessible or raising their quality – should result in improved health. Improvements in measures of education should mean that more people are making more informed choices about their health, and health 'gaps' (Marmot 2015) between those with the most and least education are generally accepted as existing both within and between countries. Levels of national income have a high measured correlation with health spending, so we would expect them to be linked with improved health, as well as having an effect independently of health spending – as countries become richer, there seems to be an improvement in their health (but perhaps subject to limits, Deaton 2015). We also know that smoking and drinking levels, at least at the individual level, affect our health.

In addition to these factors, there are political elements that influence the way health systems work. In Chapter 2, we noted that all chapters in the book include the Maleki and Hendriks measure of integrative government to attempt to capture whether particular government forms have a relationship with each of the New Giants. We might suspect that more integrative forms of government would have wider interest group involvement and participation, and so be more likely to attempt to address health inequalities (this certainly seemed to be the case for inequalities more generally as Chapter 4 found), and this will be tested in this chapter's data.

Alongside integrative government, however, there is another clear political element that frequently arises in the health policy literature that has the potential to be important. Immergut's (1992a, 1992b) hugely influential work on comparative health policy indicates that 'veto points' are of central importance to the development or blockage of new policy proposals. This idea has also been used to explain the difficulty of achieving health system change in the United States (Steinmo and Watts 1995). High numbers of veto points in the political system appear to make policymaking (and especially policy change) in an area such as health, where there are powerful interest groups present, extremely difficult. Political systems with high numbers of veto points, then, may struggle to change and adapt as the health needs of the nation change, and exploring whether or not this is the case seems an important question to consider. There is certainly a counter-argument that countries with lower numbers of veto points and highly centralized governments might end up changing healthcare policy too frequently (especially in England, Smith and Walsh 2001), and so the impact of the presence or absence of veto points on preventable mortality is an interesting question that we will attempt to unpack. In summary, the causal factors included in the analysis of this chapter are as follows:

First, in line with the findings from the OECD, but also from Deaton (2015), health expenditure is included with the general assumption that higher levels of health expenditure should lead to lower preventable mortality.

Work from the social determinants of health stresses the importance of inequality as a causal factor. Measuring inequality is, as we noted in Chapter 2, a significant challenge. Most of the research on the social determinants of health uses the post-tax and transfers 'GINI' measure of income inequality not because it necessarily captures inequality as we would like, but because it is a measure for which we can gather data for the countries that we need, and is likely to be robust in its measurement. Whatever concerns we might have about the use of the GINI coefficient, it does appear in existing research to have a central place, and so including it here makes this book more compatible with existing research, but allows it to be critically questioned through the results generated, which use different methods (cluster analysis and QCA) to those in more general use (typically based around linear models). As such, although there are concerns about the use of the GINI coefficient, it is included here, in terms of its measure of income inequality post tax and transfers, which takes account of the impact of the welfare state. Including the GINI coefficient, however, raises the question of whether the analysis is simply putting two factors that are highly correlated – income inequality and preventable mortality – on different sides of the calculation of sufficiency, and so the two will inevitably be linked to one another (although that claim might give policymakers some pause for what it might mean). However, this is not the case for two reasons.

First, QCA is not a technique based on correlations, but is instead, as Chapter 3 explained, based on finding necessary and sufficient conditions. It is possible that a high degree of correlation might mean that lower-income inequality would also be either necessary or sufficient (or both) for lower preventable mortality, but because QCA is based on conjunctions or combinations of factors, this would depend on other causal factors.

The second reason why the GINI score might not have a simple relationship with preventable mortality is that the correlation coefficient between the income GINI coefficient and the outcome measure for this chapter (see below) is -0.1745 with a p value of 0.41. As such, even in correlation terms, there is only a very weak relationship between the two.

The next factor included in the analysis attempts to capture the extent of veto points in the different political systems of countries to explore if and how this factor interacts with the others here in terms of health. There is no standard measure of the number of veto points in governments, and so a proxy measure has to be found that captures this aspect. As noted in Chapter 2, Lijphart's model of democracy has two dimensions, that of executive parties (which is strongly related to the Maleki and Hendriks integrative government measure), and its 'federal unitary' dimension. This second dimension is the more controversial of Lijphart's measures because it is made up of such a disparate collection of measures (the extent of bicameralism, constitutional rigidity, judicial review and central bank independence) that critics suggest only tangentially related to the extent or not of federalism in a government (Bormann 2010). There certainly seems to be some justification in critics' claims that these measures do not capture federalism, but they do present a range of veto points present (or not) in government systems, and so the index seems like a strong fit to capture this aspect of politics. If Immergut and other writers who stress the importance of veto points in blocking policy change governance are correct, this seems like an important factor to consider in the analysis here.

The final two factors included in the analysis are in common with the other chapters of this book, as noted in Chapter 2. The Maleki and Hendriks measure of integrative government, as noted above, is included to see whether governments which incorporate a wider range of interests leads to policymaking that is more concerned with health and wellbeing. The proportion of people with tertiary education in the country captures the relationship found in OECD research between education and life expectancy. We would expect countries with higher levels of tertiary education to have better health in terms of both being better informed about lifestyle factors linked to better health and having access to more highly skilled jobs with a stronger 'locus of control' over work, and the wellbeing benefits this seems to confer (Marmot 2012).

## OUTCOME MEASURE

The chapter's outcome measure is a composite measure, comprising the OECD preventable mortality statistic combined with a range of other OECD measures of life expectancy, along with statistics commonly used to measure how effectively healthcare systems function, including deaths from cancer and stroke mortality rates. This range of factors is often used in measures of health systems designed to capture the 'outcome' of the system as a whole (see Schneider et al. 2017). To these, a measure of the suicide rate in different countries was also included, given the rising of importance of 'deaths of despair' reported in Chapter 2. All these measures then needed to be combined into a single number to capture these different dimensions.

Producing a single factor using Principal Components Analysis did not work well, with one factor alone accounting for only 0.45 of the variance. Producing a single index always involves some compromises, so here I followed the approach of the Commonwealth Fund (Schneider et al. 2017), scaling the individual variables, and then calculating the mean of the scaled variables for each country to produce a final index value. The final values appear valid in terms of their fit with other measures (the correlation with the OECD preventable years of life lost (PYLL) measure alone is 0.8766), and the values derived appear to have both face validity in terms of largely following the ranking of countries in relation to the countries in the sample that are present in the Commonwealth Fund's international health outcome measures.

## CLUSTER ANALYSIS

The 'raw' data for each of the measures were standardized and then explored first using cluster analysis applying the Ward.D and complete clustering algorithms. The Ward.D clustering results were as follows:

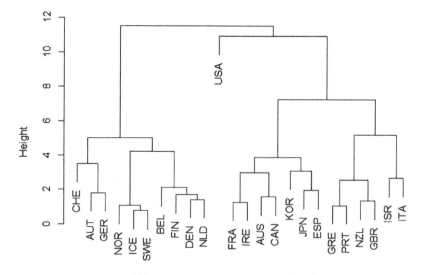

*Figure 5.1       Ward.D clustering – preventable mortality*

Reading from the top downwards, the first split in the dendrogram is between a range of Western European countries that also appeared together in the dendrogram for inequality in Chapter 4. However, there also are some key differences with the inequality dendrogram. First, France is no longer a part of the left-hand clustering, moving to the right-hand side where it appears most similar to Ireland. Second, the USA has become separated from the rest of the countries on the right-hand side of the diagram in a clear way, suggesting it is a significant outlier.

The rest of the cluster on the left-hand side of the dendrogram looks familiar from the chapter on inequality, with some small differences between the more fine-grained relationships in the clusterings for inequality (Switzerland is now closest to Austria and Germany, whereas Denmark and Finland have moved a little away from Norway and Sweden). On the right-hand side of the diagram there is the addition of France and separation of the USA, but the UK also moves into the group of 'Southern' European countries (from which Spain has become detached), with Israel also moving into that group.

The second clustering method, based on complete linkage, produces a rather different result:

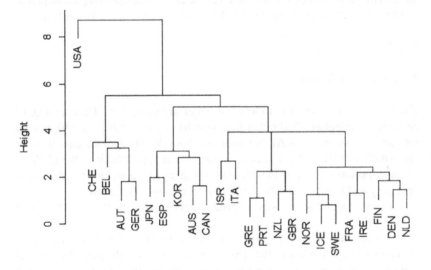

*Figure 5.2     Complete clustering – preventable mortality*

The first split in the dendrogram is between the USA and everyone else, as with Ward clustering. Below the USA, there are three broad clusters of countries. The first includes Switzerland, Belgium, Austria and Germany, which were on the left-hand side of the first clustering, but with Belgium further apart than using Ward clustering. This higher-level clustering appears to have two smaller clusters beneath it, the first including Japan, Spain, Korea, Australia and Canada, and the second fork including all the remaining countries located to the right-hand side of the dendrogram.

The right hand-side of the dendrogram includes countries that were clustered closely together using the Ward method, but here Ireland and France
are clustered with Denmark and the Netherlands (which was very much not
the case in Ward clustering). In addition, we find Israel and Italy positioned
closely together, as are Greece and Portugal and New Zealand and the UK.
However, we also find Norway, Iceland and Sweden, which were together
on the left-hand side of the Ward clustering, but here appear separate from
western and northern European countries such as Switzerland, Austria and
Belgium that were much closer to them in the Ward clustering.

As such, although there appears to be a high degree of agreement at the
more fine-grained level of clusters about which countries are most similar to
one another, at a high level the two different methods of linkage produce rather
different dendrogram structures at a more macro scale and this suggests that
the data might be more complex than was the case for inequalities in Chapter 4.

The next section examines the QCA solutions for preventable mortality.

## QCA

### Necessary Conditions

The first stage of fsQCA is to look for necessary conditions. Here a range of
possible combinations had either high consistency (at or around 0.9) or high
relevance (at or around 0.6), but none had both. It was also the case that the
combinations with the highest consistency did not appear to fit well with theoretical expectations, and so the decision was taken not to include any factors as
necessary and to proceed with the rest of the analysis on that basis.

The next stage of analysis is the production of the truth table, which can be
seen in Table 5.1.

This truth table has some interesting rows within it. The three rows with
the cases of FIN, GBR and IRE are important because, although their causal
combinations were highly consistent with high health outcomes, they were
excluded from the solution term here because of their low PRI scores, suggesting that those combinations were also associated with lower preventable health
outcomes as well. As such, a PRI threshold of 0.5 was put in place to make sure
such cases did not fall into the lower preventable mortality set.

The intermediate sufficient solution has three pathways, which can be seen
in Table 5.2.

*Table 5.1*     *Truth table – preventable mortality*

| HEALTHEXP | EDUCTERT | GINIPOST | MHINT | LJJPFU | OUT | CONSIST | PRI | CASES |
|---|---|---|---|---|---|---|---|---|
| 0 | 0 | 0 | 1 | 0 | 0 | 0.846 | 0.242 | FIN |
| 0 | 0 | 1 | 0 | 0 | 0 | 0.732 | 0.305 | GRE, NZL, PRT |
| 0 | 0 | 1 | 1 | 1 | 1 | 1.000 | 1.000 | ITA |
| 0 | 1 | 0 | 1 | 0 | 1 | 0.896 | 0.550 | ICE |
| 0 | 1 | 1 | 0 | 0 | 0 | 0.838 | 0.443 | GBR |
| 0 | 1 | 1 | 0 | 1 | 1 | 0.947 | 0.819 | JPN, KOR, ESP |
| 0 | 1 | 1 | 1 | 0 | 1 | 0.989 | 0.954 | ISR |
| 1 | 0 | 0 | 1 | 1 | 0 | 0.777 | 0.007 | AUT, GER |
| 1 | 1 | 0 | 0 | 0 | 0 | 0.884 | 0.435 | IRE |
| 1 | 1 | 0 | 0 | 1 | 0 | 0.911 | 0.217 | FRA |
| 1 | 1 | 0 | 1 | 0 | 1 | 0.840 | 0.569 | DEN, NOR, SWE |
| 1 | 1 | 0 | 1 | 1 | 0 | 0.740 | 0.296 | BEL, NLD, CHE |
| 1 | 1 | 1 | 0 | 1 | 0 | 0.755 | 0.350 | AUS, CAN, USA |

*Table 5.2        Sufficient solution – preventable mortality*

| Solution | Consistency | PRI | Coverage | Unique coverage | Cases |
|---|---|---|---|---|---|
| EDUCTERT* MHINT*~ LIJPFU | 0.868 | 0.695 | 0.457 | 0.251 | ICE, ISR, DEN, NOR, ~ SWE |
| ~HEALTHEXP *EDUCTERT *GINI*LIJPFU | 0.950 | 0.826 | 0.388 | 0.181 | JPN, KOR, ESP |
| ~HEALTHEXP* GINI*MHIN T*LIJPFU | 0.989 | 0.947 | 0.257 | 0.050 | ITA |

Note: Overall solution consistency 0.888, Coverage 0.689

The first pathway is a combination of higher tertiary education, highly integrative government, and a lower score on the Lijphart 'Federal-Unitary' scale, which here equates to a lower federalism score, and so lower numbers of political veto points. It has a consistency of 0.868, a coverage of 0.457 and a unique coverage of 0.251. It includes the cases of Iceland, Israel, Denmark, Norway and Sweden. This solution has the highest coverage and unique coverage, but with one case deviant for consistency – that of Denmark.

The second pathway is a combination of lower health expenditure, higher tertiary education and higher income inequality, and has a higher score on the Lijphart 'Federal-Unity' suggesting, in turn, higher numbers of political veto points. It covers the cases of Japan, Korea and Spain, but with Korea deviant for consistency. This pathway has a coverage score of 0.388 and a unique coverage score of 0.181.

The final solution pathway covers one country only (Italy) and consists of lower health expenditure, higher GINI, highly integrative government and lower numbers of veto points. It has the lowest unique coverage score as we would expect (0.050) as it covers only one case.

As noted above, there are two cases deviant for consistency (Denmark and Korea), but there are also two cases deviant for coverage (and so missing from the solution above, but having a higher health index score) – those countries are Australia and Switzerland.

We can illustrate that Denmark and Korea are deviant for consistency by showing the relationship between the higher preventable solution and the set membership scores of countries against that outcome.

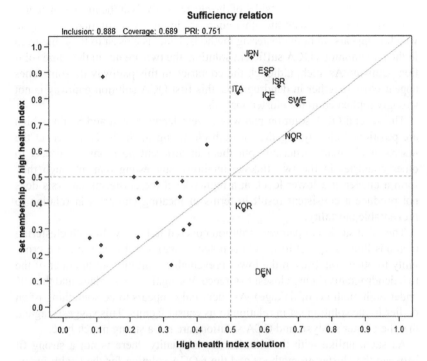

*Figure 5.3    Preventable mortality sufficiency relation*

The conservative sufficient solution has four pathways, adding an additional pathway to the sufficient solution combining ~HEALTHEXP*EDUCTERT*MHINT*~LIJPFU for ICE and ISR only, to those above. The parsimonious solution has two pathways only. The first is ~HEALTHEXP*GINI*LIJPFU covering Italy, Japan, Korea and Spain (so bringing Italy into the solution for the three other countries), and with the other pathway identical to the first of the intermediate solution.

## COMPARISON OF CLUSTER ANALYSIS AND QCA

Finally, we can consider the relationship between the sufficient solutions and the cluster analysis.

The first QCA solution pathway covers Iceland, Israel, Denmark, Norway and Sweden. Of these countries, Norway, Iceland and Sweden are closely clustered together in both dendrograms, and so these countries appear to be strongly linked however we look at the data. Denmark is a case that is deviant for consistency in the QCA analysis, which is interesting in that although it tends to appear on the same 'side' of the cluster analysis at the macro level, it is not closely clustered with the other countries in the QCA solution pathway in which it appears. In both clustering methods, Israel is closest to Italy, but even in the parsimonious QCA sufficient solution, the two are not in the same solution pathway. As such, although the countries in this pathway do sometimes appear close together in dendrograms, this first QCA solution pathway is not strongly replicated in the cluster analysis.

The second QCA solution pathway covers Japan, Korea and Spain, which are positioned closely together in both clustering methods. However, at the macro level, their clusterings put them in different positions in respect to other countries in the two linkage methods, suggesting that although they form a cluster at a lower level, at a higher level the clustering analysis does not produce a consistent result in terms of locating countries in relation to preventable mortality.

The third sufficient pathway solution covered Italy only. In both clustering methods Italy is closest to Israel (as noted above), but it is not in close proximity to other countries in the lower preventable mortality set in either of the two dendrograms (being closest to Greece, Portugal, New Zealand and the UK under both methods of linkage). As such, Italy appears to be something of an outlier in the solution set in relation to its causal factors. This suggests, again, that the cluster analysis and QCA solutions are not a strong match here.

As such, unlike with the solution for inequality, there is not a strong fit between the clustering methods and the fsQCA solution for the health index. Part of the reason for this is that, although countries tend to cluster together consistently across the different solutions in terms of their locations to others at lower levels in both clustering linkage methods, there is less agreement at the higher level where larger clusters are formed. This would suggest that the data are more ambiguous in terms of which countries are closest to one another beyond smaller-scale clusters. The data for preventable mortality do not form patterns at this higher level of abstraction, which is consistent with the QCA sufficient solutions in the same way as for inequality.

## DISCUSSION

There were no necessary conditions for lower preventable mortality. That there are no necessary conditions suggests sufficient solution pathways that exhibit strong equifinality, where there are routes to lower preventable mortality where different pathways might have causal conditions that might contradict one another, as there are no factors that must appear in solutions.

The first intermediate solution pathway had the highest coverage and unique coverage, and was made up of higher levels of tertiary education, an integrative form of government and a lower score on Lijphart's 'Federal-Unity' scale, so lower numbers of potential political veto points. This solution includes a range of countries that are highly educated (so high skill), and are politically represented by government institutions that are integrative (so include a wide range of interests) but also where power is relatively centralized. This combination of factors represents the working of democracies in which there are wider opportunities to contribute than in less inclusive governments, where people are also more likely to be well informed because of their higher education levels, but where centralized governments with fewer veto points, once policy has been decided through deliberation, are able to act with few veto points.

It is worth noting that this solution helps expand on the 'veto points' argument from Immergut. In the first solution pathway we find governments that have wide inclusivity (which would suggest vetoes might occur) but are lower in terms of federalism – so have fewer political veto points. Immergut's thesis was that a large number of veto points would prevent health policy change. What this pathway suggests is perhaps more nuanced: that governments able to incorporate a range of different views in policymaking (highly integrative governments), and then implement them in a unified way (lower in terms of federalism), are the most consistent in achieving preventable mortality. Countries that have less integrative, highly centralized governments in contrast, may be able to change health policy relatively easily (Wilsford 1994), but if that policy was not consensually agreed, will find that they struggle in terms of implementation (Exworthy, Berney and Powell 2002).

However, as already noted, there is more than one route to achieving lower preventable mortality. The second pathway comprises lower health expenditure, higher tertiary education (the only factor in common with the first pathway), higher income inequality and a higher score on Lijphart's Federal–Unitary government scale, suggesting a federal government with more veto points. This combination of factors is an unusual one: it suggests both lower health expenditure and higher income inequality can be compatible with lower preventable mortality, when combined with higher tertiary education and a more federal government, albeit in a smaller range of countries than the first solution pathway. This is rather unexpected, but the range of countries does include Spain, which was ranked in 2019 as the best healthcare system in the world,[1] and is certainly an important combination of factors.

The third solution pathway overlaps considerably with the second (and is merged with the second in some sufficient solutions as we have seen) and combines lower health expenditure, higher income inequality and highly integrative government (which replaces higher tertiary education in the second pathway) along with a higher score for federal government. It covers Italy only. However, the combination at the root of the second and third pathways – lower health expenditure, higher income inequality and higher federal government – does appear to present an alternative route to lower preventable mortality than the first pathway.

The sufficient solutions have two cases that are deviant for consistency – where countries that are included in the solution but have higher preventable mortality – and two cases that are deviant for coverage (so are missing from the sufficient solutions although they achieve lower preventable mortality).

Denmark is the first case deviant for consistency. Denmark is often regarded, in comparative studies, as having a great deal in common with Sweden and sometimes Norway and Iceland (the latter for political reasons), and so it is unsurprising to find it in the same cluster as those two countries here. Denmark appears on the same truth table row as Norway and Sweden, but scores notice-ably worse on the health index than its two neighbours. Indeed, Denmark has a calibrated score of 0.12 on the combined health index – the second worst of all the countries in the sample – compared with 0.64 for Norway and 0.77 for Sweden. Denmark's poor result appears to be a result of an historical legacy that is a little different to that of Norway and Sweden, and is based on having very high smoking rates as recently as 2000, as well as the highest alcohol consumption in the European Union. Denmark appears to have a strong healthcare system with good access, but with significant challenges due to cancer and cardiovascular diseases, linked explicitly to the formerly very high smoking and drinking habits of its people (OECD 2017a). Although Denmark has lower levels of income inequality, there also seems to be significant differ-ences in behavioural factors between the richest and poorest, which contribute to Denmark's poor score for preventable mortality. The positive news is that Denmark appears to be gradually dealing with its poor health inheritance.

If Denmark's health problems appear to be related to a legacy of heavy smoking (now falling) and heavy drinking (still present, but with significant differences between social groups), South Korea scores relatively poorly (0.37 on the health index) despite having amongst the best cancer care in the world. Korea's health problems are in its suicide rate (which is the highest in the OECD) and with a high (relative to countries) rate of smoking, with Korea being rather late in introducing public health measures around the latter compared with many other nations in the sample. The suicide rate is clearly a significant problem, and appears to be especially prevalent amongst the elderly poor, and then particularly in the elderly, rural poor (Kim et al. 2010). Many of the problems of the poor and elderly appear to stem from the lack of social assistance for that group. It is clear that South Korea needs to look hard at this problem; it is deviant for consistency here, with the evidence from the research suggesting it could achieve far better preventable mortality if it were to invest in this vulnerable group.

As well as cases deviant for consistency, there are two cases deviant for coverage. The first of these, Australia, is, in health terms, an extraordinary one. Australia is, in comparative terms, a country that appears to be able to confound expectations across a range of causal factors and still produce strong health outcomes (Greener 2021b). The robust health of Australia's people, despite having a range of factors that do not appear to support such high achievement, mark it as an exception in almost every comparative measure of both health and welfare systems, but one that still faces significant challenges in relation to its indigenous peoples, who have outcomes that are far worse than the white population. Australia may be an exception due to good diet, or climate, or general lifestyle, but in terms of its pattern of general causal factors, which it shares with the United States of America (which has the poorest of all countries in terms of preventable mortality) and Canada, it does not seem to offer reliable lessons for other countries.

The second case deviant for coverage is that of Switzerland. Switzerland has amongst the best health outcomes in the sample, achieving a calibrated score of 0.88. Switzerland appears on the same truth table row as Netherlands and Belgium, but, in terms of preventable mortality, outperforms them both by some margin (the other two countries have scores below 0.5). Switzerland's pattern of causal factors is HEALTHEXP*EDUCTERT*~GINI*MHINT*LIJPFU. This pattern combines higher health expenditure with higher tertiary education, lower income inequality, highly integrative government and highly federal government (so higher number of political veto points), and is arguably closest to the pattern in Denmark, Norway and Sweden – but with those countries having less-federal forms of government (so lower numbers of veto points in implementation terms). Switzerland, famously, has highly decentralized cantons with considerable autonomy; however, whereas such a structure appears to work well in Switzerland, it seems to struggle more in the contexts of Belgium and the Netherlands. One factor here is the excellence of the Swiss healthcare system, which is amongst the best in the world (Schneider et al. 2017). Another factor is that Switzerland is one of the richest nations, and despite its reputation as being expensive, has relatively low income inequality. Perhaps, rather than explaining why Switzerland is a case deviant for coverage, the key question might be why the Netherlands and Belgium are not doing better, given they share Switzerland's causal factors, as well as having other causal factors that have the potential for strong health performance. Perhaps Switzerland's cantons are able to act to support the health of their local people in ways that local government is less able to in the Netherlands and Belgium.

The third case worth additional discussion is that of Italy. Italy appears on the truth table on a row by itself. Italy's causal pattern is ~HEALTHEXP*~EDUCTERT*GINI*MHINT*LIJPFU. It shares its first three factors with Greece, New Zealand and Portugal, but its last two with Austria, Germany, Belgium, the Netherlands and Switzerland. Italy spends relatively little on healthcare, has a lower number of people with tertiary education, and higher income inequality. These factors alone appear to suggest it might do poorly in respect of preventable mortality. Politically it is integrative, but also highly federal, and as we have noted, only Switzerland has that combination of factors and is really successful in having lower preventable mortality. Why does Italy appear to succeed when it has so many factors apparently not in its favour?

Italy has a very strong healthcare system (ranked 2nd in the world by the WHO in 2000, World Health Organization 2000) but is also consistently highlighted in international studies because of the good diet of its people. It also seems that Italians began to stop smoking earlier than in many other nations. This combination of factors appears to mean that, despite so many factors counting against it, Italy is still able to succeed in terms of preventable mortality.

Finally, as noted in the cluster analysis, countries consistently form the same clusters at a more granular level than they did in Chapter 4. This suggests that, although there are clear groupings of countries, they do not form consistent patterns at a higher level, and do not correspond as closely to the QCA sufficient solutions. This means that equifinality is stronger in the data on preventable mortality. Although there are pathways that combine the causal factors in the chapter to produce sufficient solutions, there are no necessary conditions, and there are at least some causal factors that are contradictory between the sufficient solution pathways (although, of course, combined with different causal factors).

The causal recipe for achieving lower preventable mortality is therefore more complex than achieving lower inequality, although higher tertiary education is present in two of the three pathways, as is highly integrative government, which reproduces the findings from Chapter 4. What is perhaps remarkable is that higher income inequality is also present in two of the solution pathways, which again emphasizes the importance of considering causation conjunctionally. Higher income inequality does not cause preventable mortality. It is the combination of the other factors present that allows lower preventable mortality to still be achieved *despite* the presence of higher income inequality in the second and third solution pathways. Equally, the lower levels of health expenditure in the second and third pathways appear to require a more federal form of government with higher numbers of veto points in order to achieve the same goal.

## CONCLUSION

At the time of this chapter's writing (June 2021), the world is still in the middle of the global pandemic. The factors presented in this chapter clearly correspond with more 'normal' times, to which we all look forward to returning. I have published work that considers the 'first wave' response to the pandemic and tries to pick out patterns of causal factors that were clinically important (Greener 2021a) as well as exploring the process of governmental decision-making in the United Kingdom in finer detail (King-Hill, Greener and Powell 2021). It seems remiss not to consider the pandemic in a chapter concerned with preventable mortality. At the same time, COVID-19 is not the main focus of this book, and preventable mortality has taken on an entirely new dimension in the last 18 months, based more on the development of 'excess mortality' statistics that attempt to capture the effect of the spread of the virus. These statistics are still not at the stage where they are comparable, being produced in different ways in different countries; and beyond July 2020, countries have also experienced 'peaks' of virus spread at different times from one another. It also seems that the virus is still developing and new variants appearing: at the time of writing, the UK has been through a peak of the 'Essex' variant, and is struggling with another new variant that was first identified in India.

As such, although COVID-19 will clearly dominate our world for some time to come, I have not identified it as a New Giant. I have, however, included an additional chapter at the end of the book that explores the extent to which the countries that appear to do well in confronting the New Giants, also responded well to the pandemic.

Looking beyond COVID-19, it is crucial to consider why some countries do so much better than others in dealing with preventable mortality. This chapter has contributed to this debate by considering not only factors that come imme-diately to mind in relation to this (such as health expenditure and inequality levels), but also preventable mortality in relation to processes of political decision-making. As outlined above, Immergut's work strongly suggests that veto points prevent health policy change (Immergut 1992a). What we have found in our sufficient solution is a clear divide, between countries such as Norway and Sweden, which have integrative government, but with few veto points once policy has been decided upon, and Japan, Spain and Italy, which have a highly federal form, and still manage to achieve lower preventable mortality. The relationship between preventable mortality and government type is complex, but there do seem to be pathways of factors that combine to increase the chance of success. Of the countries that are successful, a small number (in particular Iceland, Norway and Sweden) were also in the sufficient solution set for lower inequality in Chapter 4, and so seem to have found ways of combatting both of the New Giants we have considered so far. As the book develops, it will continue to consider the extent to which solutions for the New Giants overlap or diverge, before returning to this issue again in the book's conclusion.

It is also the case, however, that some countries with higher levels of ine-quality have lower levels of preventable mortality, suggesting that it is possible to have one without the other. This means that there are significant differences between the combinations of factors in sufficient solution QCA pathways, and this shows in the cluster analysis solutions, which are consistent when consid-ered at the lower, country-by-country level, but at higher levels of aggregation there are far greater differences, both between cluster linkage methods and between cluster linkage methods and QCA solutions, than in Chapter 4.

The next chapter moves on to consider concerns about the crisis of demo-cratic government. Which countries have the most robust democracies, and which appear to be struggling?

## NOTE

1. According to the Bloomberg Health Efficiency Index, https://www.bloomberg
   .com/news/articles/2019-02-24/spain-tops-italy-as-world-s-healthiest-nation
   -while-u-s-slips (accessed on 9 November 2021).

# 6.    The crisis of democracy

## INTRODUCTION – A CRISIS OF DEMOCRACY?

For a brief time at the end of the 1980s, there was a period when a kind of Western Triumphalism seemed to be prevailing in which there were claims that a liberal form of democratic government was now settled as being the dominant model of governance in the world. Fukuyama's rhetorical claim about the 'End of History' (Fukuyama 2012) was based on the decline of the Soviet Union and the successful combination of capitalism and democratic governmental institutions that had triumphed through the Cold War. As the countries of Eastern Europe established their own identities, they began to hold elections, and it seemed as if it was only a matter of time before the rest of the non-democratic world followed suit. American politicians, in particular, were keen to link 'democracy' with 'freedom', providing the justification for a more interventionist foreign policy (for the USA, but also bringing in other countries as well) in which armed interventions could remove dictators in the name of bringing new freedoms to the people of those countries.

The road from 1989 to the early 2020s has, however, been one in which democracy has been repeatedly claimed to be in a 'crisis' (Barber 2004; Crouch 2004; Runciman 2018; Van Reybrouck 2016) of one kind or another.

The most obvious manifestations of these trends are well documented. In 2016 the United States of America elected as president a businessman and reality television star who proceeded to barrage the world with statements of dubious voracity, with *The Washington Post*'s count being over 30,500 misleading claims in his four years in office. Trump made extensive use of social media platforms to announce his views with little apparent regard for their truthfulness.

Also in 2016, the United Kingdom voted to leave the European Union. The referendum campaign that preceded the vote was one in which the Leave campaign made its case based on misleading claims about how the money spent on the European Union could be used elsewhere. It was not represented by the leaders of any mainstream political party, and so no one was held to account for the claims that were made (indeed the Vote Leave website was removed the day after the referendum). Misleading posters appeared concerning immigration. A Labour MP was stabbed to death in her constituency office. On

the 'Remain' side, the government sent out leaflets to every household rec-
ommending them to vote to stay in the EU, but seemed reluctant to make any
positive case for that request, instead focusing the campaign on the dreadful
effects they claimed would happen if the UK were to leave. Despite the widespread leafleting, and with all major political parties asking people to vote to
Remain, over half those who voted, voted to leave. The end result was less an
exercise in informed democracy, and instead one based around fear-mongering
(Shipman 2016).

The roots of both the election of Trump and the Leave EU campaigns ran
deeper than either of the events in themselves. In the United States, Thomas
Frank (2016) has shown how the Democrat Party liberal elite became detached
from its working-class base, no longer protecting low-skill workers, and
instead having a strategy based around higher education participation that
many 'blue collar' workers felt they had no part in. Globalized supply chains
meant that home jobs moved overseas and income levels remained static (or
even declined) for the poorest. Many of those on lower income groups found
themselves with fewer employment rights, but on the same real pay as twenty
years earlier, and saw little on offer from their representative politicians inspir-
ing them to remain loyal (Frank 2007). The growth of the internet gave many
people ready-made explanations for their woes, which included blaming immigrants, special interest groups that the Democrats supported, and demands for
a different politics demanding to 'Make America Great Again'.

In the UK, unskilled workers also saw their incomes stagnate, and the
mainstream news, increasingly owned by non-resident magnates, presented
stories (and even daytime television programmes) about welfare 'scroungers'
and claims of open borders leading to widespread benefit fraud from people
from overseas. Immigrants were, perhaps, showing more than a little contradiction, also blamed for taking jobs from British people (Garthwaite 2011).
The Labour government of 1997–2010 seemed to increasingly lose touch with
their traditional working-class voters, increasingly losing them to both extreme
right political parties (where immigration was blamed) or to the Conservative
Party, which has now been in government, first in coalition, and then by itself,
since 2010.

Disaffection with politics from working-class groups, calls for increased
nationalism, combined with the use of the internet and news media to spread
narratives of blame, has created a toxic environment that is not unique to the
UK and USA. Far-right political parties have seen their voter numbers rise
across Europe. There has been a decline in trust in governments almost across
the world (Wilkinson and Pickett 2010).

Van Reybrouck (2016) argues that our election-based voting systems are
actually undermining democracy, with politicians having to present complex
issues in soundbites, amplified by the presence of a media that cannot deal in

any kind of complexity, and creating the space for populists such as Trump, but also in Europe, Burlesconi and Le Pen. Van Reybrouck argues that we need to separate elections from democracy, and move towards a representative form of democracy in which sortition, effectively the random selection of those who govern us, is used far more extensively. Although Van Reybrouck's solution may appear radical, it is a logical extension of his main argument. However, it is also the case that some countries appear to have stronger democratic governance than many of those in his examples, and we can still learn from them.

Achen and Bartels (2016) explore the crisis of democracy from a different angle, highlighting confusions over what people mean by 'democracy', and points to the apparent contradiction between large numbers of people in the United States, for example, claiming that democracy is important for the nation's success, while at the same time suggesting that the government is run by 'big interests'. Achen and Bartels point to a range of studies suggesting that voters are not very informed in their decision-making and claim that 'election outcomes are mostly just erratic reflections of the current balance of partisan loyalties in a given political system' (p.508). Equally, with strong relevance to the pandemic, they point to how ineffectively blame is attributed by the public when things go wrong in their countries, with misunderstandings of events and short-term time horizons being common.

Although Achen and Bartels are strong on critique (and their critiques go much wider than there is space to report here), they also suggest that democracy may still be the least-worst form of government as it eventually tends to lead to the governing party being changed. Incumbents appear to grow increasingly unpopular over time, leading to the momentum for government to be refreshed and changed. Achen and Bartels also suggest that there seem to be normative limits on political behaviour that are likely to result in voter alienation (although, again, it could certainly be argued that many of these constraints seem to have at least weakened in the USA and UK). Achen and Bartels do suggest, however, that democracy is likely to work better in more equal societies, as, in that context, governing elites are less likely to be isolated from the rest of the population. They also suggest that there should be limits on lobbying and interest-group financial contributions to political parties. These suggestions appear generally sensible, but they have been difficult to implement because of the entrenchment of political lobby groups (Reich 2009).

A different form of democratic critique comes from theorists of deliberative democracy, with Dryzek (for example, 2000) perhaps being the most prolific and influential. The argument is that the problem with democracy is its deliberative elements are in danger of being lost, and what will reinvigorate our democratic processes is the opportunity for the public to have real and informed participation in democratic processes. In this view, voting is a part of democracy, but by no means enough. The distinctive part of deliberative democracy is the opportunity for citizens to engage with others in decision-making, and having the opportunity to reflect and change their minds as a result. This deliberation, Dryzek suggests, can act as a curb on the influence of political interests, as well as helping to bridge cross-interest divides with citizens encouraged to come to agreements about what should happen, even if they cannot find consensus, through the use of a range of deliberative mechanisms and practices.

For Dryzek, then, it is crucial that people are able to participate in political processes, to engage with one another in the public sphere, and that this will result in better decision-making for us all. Political participation here is a good in itself, in that it leads to people becoming more informed, as well as forming a link between participating in decisions and working to make those decisions work better. The use of democratic institutions such as citizen's juries presents the opportunity for people to participate in decision-making and engage in a process of both substantive and political learning, and is also strongly advocated as a means of renewing faith in democratic processes.

Looking across the critiques presented here, there are debates around the definition of democracy, as well as about the possible ways of dealing with the challenges it is now facing. The next section explores the causal factors that the chapter will consider, as well as how the outcome measure for this chapter was selected.

## CAUSAL FACTORS

Looking comparatively, several key factors appear to be part of the crisis of democracy. As noted above, wage stagnation for the poorest appears to be a key factor, but it is largely present across the countries in the sample here, and so cannot really be used to differentiate between them, even if it is a crucial cause.

The causal factors that will be included in the chapter are based on complex causal chains, perhaps more complex than in the other chapters in the book. They are as follows:

First, there is the complex relationship between globalization and the crisis of democracy. As noted in Chapter 1, Giddens viewed globalization as potentially creating a positive force in which the citizens of countries would demand change in their countries as a result of knowing more about the world due to improved global communications. The internet especially has allowed for people from across the world to communicate in the way Giddens suggested, but has also clearly had a darker side that has links to the spreading of disinformation and to rather less mutual understanding, as outlined in the events of 2016 outlined in the previous section.

As globalization plays such an important role in the work of theorists such as Beck and Giddens, including this factor makes a great deal of sense. However, globalization can be measured in a variety of different ways, and the causal links between those aspects need to be carefully thought through. First, globalization is often measured in terms of international trade flows (Babones 2013) and, as we have seen above, trade flows are clearly part of the story told in relation to political disaffection, especially in the United States. However, this is only one aspect of it. A second key aspect is in relation to the spread of technology, and this clearly also needs to be comparatively measured, especially in terms of internet usage. However, it also needs to take account of the influence of multinational corporations as they are part of the narrative presented around the impact of globalization on democracy. The KOF Globalization Index includes all of these aspects, and so, as with Chapter 4 on inequality, is a good measure to include here. Including this factor allows us to explore whether higher levels of globalization are linked to countries with lower levels of democracy.

The second factor included in this chapter is GDP per capita. This factor is included to try to assess whether richer countries tend to have higher levels of democracy. GDP per capita is an almost universally included control variable in standard macrocomparative analysis, and that is also the case in many comparative studies of democracy. As such, it is included here to link to existing research, but also because there is contradictory research pointing to the links between democracy and the level of income present in a country. At a global level, richer countries tend to be more democratic. However, within such countries (which is the sample here), there may be another effect in which 'affluence' leads to increased political apathy (as suggested by the work of Galbraith and Offer already reviewed). Crisis events can still lead to significant change (which will be interesting to consider in the light of the Coronavirus pandemic), but there is certainly the possibility that, as people become richer, they have less incentive to engage with politics. We have already seen that, despite average incomes rising since the 1980s, incomes for those at the bottom end have not. As a result, those experiencing no increase in their standard of living may regard themselves excluded from political debate, and so disengage for different reasons. Including GDP per capita therefore allows us to explore how debates between levels of national income and democracy play out in the data.

As well as considering national income alone, however, it is also important to consider the distribution of income within an economy. As such, there is a strong case for including a measure of income inequality on the assumption that higher levels of inequality may lead to less democratic engagement. As with other chapters, we include the GINI coefficient here, both as a means of making the book's findings more compatible with existing research, but also because the GINI measure, despite its failings, does appear to have a link to a range of social 'ills' (Marmot 2015; Wilkinson and Pickett 2010) and so is worth including even if it does not entirely capture the dimensions of inequality more generally.

Finally, the chapter includes the two factors present in other chapters. Both again have clear links to our outcome. Higher levels of tertiary education should mean that the citizenry is more informed and able to engage in democratic processes. As governments have put such a premium on increasing the number of graduates, has this improved the functioning of democracy (as its advocates would suggest it should, Nussbaum 2010) or polarized politics and society further (as the Frank critique above would suggest)?

The Maleki and Hendriks measure of integrative government suggests a hypothesis, in relation to democracy, that more highly integrative governmental systems should lead to improved democracy. First-past-the-post electoral systems with few political parties will tend to exclude substantial minorities from political engagement while parties they did not vote for are in power. More representational governmental electoral and governance mechanisms should offer more opportunity for involvement through either interest representation or by increased chances to participate in governmental coalitions.

As such, the causal factors for this chapter are globalization, national income per capita, inequality, and the measures of tertiary education participation and integrative government used in the rest of the book.

## OUTCOME MEASURE

Achieving a single outcome factor for the extent of democracy in a country is not straightforward. The Polity IV measure is widely used in global studies, but it has been widely critiqued (Babones 2013) and shows relatively little variation amongst the countries in the sample in this book, so is not used here.

Looking more widely, the measure that appears to more accurately capture the concerns expressed in relation to a potential crisis of democracy is most closely expressed by the Economist Democracy Index.[1] The Economist Index includes a range of elements that capture dimensions of the concerns expressed around democracy (measuring whether elections are fair, how well the government functions, the level of political participation, a measure of the political culture, and the extent of civil liberties), while at the same time showing some variation in its gradings (several countries in the sample are currently graded as 'flawed democracies' including Korea, Japan, USA, Israel, Belgium, Italy and Greece). The Economist measure, as well as presenting an overall index, also includes full details of the component parts within it, showing a strong degree of transparency and allowing the overall index to be disaggregated (which is needed for us to 'balance' cluster analysis between causal factors and outcome measures).

## CLUSTER ANALYSIS

The Ward clustering of the 'raw' data for this chapter is produced below.

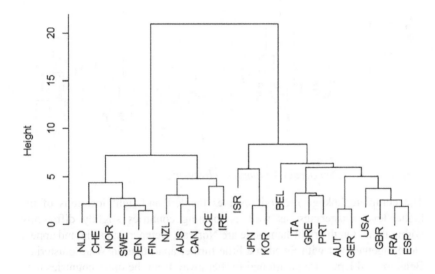

*Figure 6.1      Democracy – Ward clustering*

Looking at this clustering, and working down from the top of the dendrogram, the left-hand fork includes Scandinavian countries (plus Switzerland and the Netherlands), plus New Zealand, Australia and Canada, and then finally Iceland and Ireland. The right-hand fork combines Israel with Japan and Korea, and Belgium with Italy, Greece and Portugal. The next group of countries on the right-hand side clustering is Austria and Germany, which appear to be closest to the USA, then finally the UK, France and Spain. Both sides of the dendrogram are mixed in terms of their geographical spread, but with some regional clusterings at lower levels – there seems to be a Scandinavian cluster, one for South Europe, and smaller regional clusterings such as New Zealand and Australia, and Austria and Germany.

*Welfare states in the 21st century*

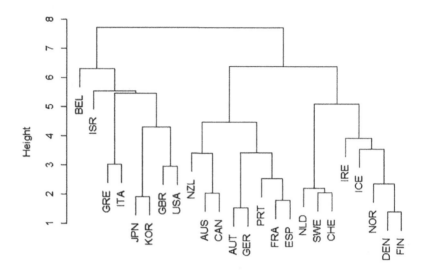

*Figure 6.2    Democracy – complete clustering*

The complete linkage method reverses the left and right locations of the higher-level clusterings, as well as locating countries slightly differently within them. On the right-hand side are Norway, Denmark and Finland appear close together, but with Sweden a little further apart than in Ward clustering. Belgium and Israel are positioned further away from the other countries than under Ward.D linkage. Australia, Canada and New Zealand are still close together, but in complete linkage are now close to Portugal, France and Spain, as well as to Austria and Germany, with these latter five countries located on the other 'fork' under Ward.D clustering. This move of these five countries from the Ward.D linkage produces a less 'balanced' dendrogram at the top level.

Both linkage methods suggest either a wide or narrower Scandinavian cluster (Norway, Denmark and Finland, with or without Sweden), another cluster between Australia, Canada and New Zealand, others between Iceland and Ireland, Japan and Korea, Austria and Germany, Greece and Italy, and Spain and France, with the UK and the USA also located near to one another in the dendrograms. How do these clusterings of countries fit with the solutions generated by QCA?

# QCA

The first stage of fsQCA is to identify necessary conditions. A range of possible conditions were explored, but with a combination of ~GINI+GDPCAP (lower levels of income inequality or higher levels of income per capita) having high consistency (0.895) and high relevance (0.689) as well as fitting with existing theory (lower inequality or higher national income seem like possible routes to a strong democracy).

This combination of factors is also credible theoretically. It is certainly hard to see how higher levels of inequality could underpin a healthy democracy, as higher inequality is likely to be associated with, as we saw in Chapter 4 a range of social problems that would undermine democratic governance. It would also be logical to say that lower levels of inequality mean there would be more of a sense of collective fate for a country, which was a key element in Marshall's work exploring the relationship between citizenship and social class (Marshall 1950). It is important to note, though, that the two necessary conditions are combined with a '+', so in set-theoretical terms, an 'OR'. Here a strong democratic score is related to either lower income inequality OR higher levels of GDP, suggesting that there may be a degree of complex causality, although perhaps less than we saw in Chapter 5 (where there were no necessary conditions). Higher levels of GDP go against work from Offer and Galbraith suggesting that richer countries generate 'affluence' or 'contentment' leading to lower democratic participation, but the opposite could also be true – living in a richer nation might give people greater freedoms to be engaged in political life. Exploring how these two factors combine with other causal factors might give us valuable clues as to how they are playing out in sufficient solutions.

The next step is the construction of the truth table, which can be seen in Table 6.1.

The truth table has a couple of rows that require some explanation. The second row from the top (Austria and Germany) is close to achieving the 0.8 threshold, but it was excluded as the PRI score is below 0.5, and so these two countries were treated as being in the lower democracy solution. Towards the middle of the truth table, France has a consistency score of 0.801, but a PRI score of 0.399, so the decision was also taken to exclude France from the sufficient solution on the grounds of there being the presence of a simultaneous subset relation, with France's set of causal factors appearing in both the set of highly democratic countries, as well as the lower democratic countries as well.

This truth table is then used to calculate sufficient solutions, once counterfactual rows that have the opposite of the necessary condition were excluded. Directional expectations, in line with the review of causal factors above, were those of higher tertiary education (as a more educated public should be able to

*Table 6.1*    *Truth table – democracy*

| EDUCTERT | GINIPOST | KOFGLOBI9 | MHINT | GDPCAP | OUT | CONSISTENCY | PRI | CASES |
|---|---|---|---|---|---|---|---|---|
| 0 | 0 | 1 | 1 | 0 | 1 | 0.875 | 0.579 | FIN |
| 0 | 0 | 1 | 1 | 1 | 0 | 0.795 | 0.469 | AUT, GER |
| 0 | 1 | 0 | 0 | 0 | 0 | 0.618 | 0.229 | GRE, NZL |
| 0 | 1 | 0 | 1 | 0 | 0 | 0.682 | 0.058 | ITA |
| 0 | 1 | 1 | 0 | 0 | 0 | 0.599 | 0.011 | PRT |
| 1 | 0 | 0 | 1 | 1 | 1 | 1.000 | 1.000 | ICE |
| 1 | 0 | 1 | 0 | 0 | 0 | 0.801 | 0.399 | FRA |
| 1 | 0 | 1 | 0 | 1 | 1 | 0.953 | 0.859 | IRE |
| 1 | 0 | 1 | 1 | 1 | 1 | 0.895 | 0.799 | BEL, DEN, NLD, NOR, SWE, CHE |
| 1 | 1 | 0 | 0 | 0 | 0 | 0.625 | 0.242 | JPN, KOR |
| 1 | 1 | 0 | 0 | 1 | 1 | 0.849 | 0.581 | AUS, USA |
| 1 | 1 | 0 | 1 | 0 | 0 | 0.734 | 0.067 | ISR |
| 1 | 1 | 1 | 0 | 0 | 0 | 0.719 | 0.256 | CAN, ESP, GBR |

participate more democratically) and higher GDP per capita (in line with the necessary condition above). The intermediate sufficient solution can be seen in Table 6.2.

*Table 6.2       Sufficient solution – democracy*

| Solution | Consistency | PRI | Coverage | Unique coverage | Cases |
|---|---|---|---|---|---|
| EDUCTERT *~GINI*K OFGLOB* GDPCAP | 0.884 | 0.786 | 0.519 | 0.017 | IRE, BEL, DEN, NLD, NOR, SWE, CHE |
| EDUCTERT ~GINI*MHI NT*GDPCAP | 0.906 | 0.829 | 0.515 | 0.054 | ICE, BEL, DEN, NLD, NOR, SWE, CHE |
| EDUCTERT* GINI*~KOFG LOB*~MHIN T*GDPCAP | 0.849 | 0.581 | 0.288 | 0.072 | AUS, USA |
| ~EDUCTERT *~GINI*K OFGLOB* MHINT*~GD PCAL | 0.875 | 0.579 | 0.259 | 0.065 | FIN |

*Note*: Solution consistency 0.846, coverage 0.717

The intermediate sufficient solution for higher levels of democracy has four pathways, but with considerable overlap between them (hence the low unique coverage scores for all of them).

The first pathway combines higher tertiary education with lower income inequality, higher globalization and higher GDP per capita. This pathway has a high coverage (0.519), but low unique coverage (as do all the solution pathways because of the extent of their overlap), and covers the cases of Ireland, Belgium, Denmark, the Netherlands, Norway, Sweden and Switzerland. However, Belgium is deviant for consistency.

The second pathway combines higher tertiary education, lower GINI, higher integrative government and higher GDP per capita. The solution therefore exchanges the higher globalization in the first solution pathway for highly integrative government, and in doing so loses Ireland from the solution but introduces Iceland. All the other countries from the first pathway are present, though. That means Belgium is again deviant for consistency.

The third and fourth pathways cover only three countries between them, but with the USA deviant for consistency in the third pathway, so reducing the solution to covering one country with a higher democracy score (Australia).

There are two countries deviant for coverage in the solution – New Zealand and Canada – and so are rated as highly democratic despite not appearing in the QCA solution.

The first two pathways, because of their high coverage and strong overlap, appear to be the most empirically important. Looking across the four pathways, three have higher tertiary education and higher GDP per capita in place, and

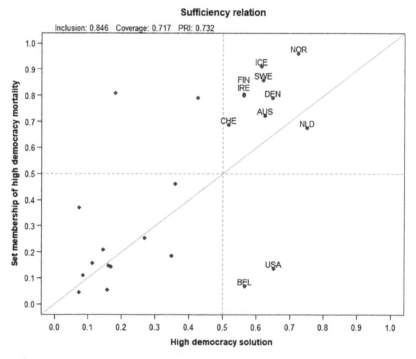

*Figure 6.3      Sufficient solution – democracy*

three of the four also have lower income inequality. The status of the USA and Belgium as cases deviant for consistency is clear from the chart plotting the higher democracy solution against the set membership for higher democracy. The conservative solution is identical to the intermediate solution presented above. The parsimonious solution has three pathways, with EDUCTERT*~GINI*GDPCAP covering the first two pathways of the intermediate solution (and so all the countries included in both of those pathways including both Iceland and Ireland), with ~MHINT*GDPCAP making up the second pathway and covering Ireland, Australia and the USA, and the third pathway having the same combination of factors to cover Finland.

## COMPARISON OF CLUSTER ANALYSIS AND QCA SOLUTIONS

If we compare the sufficient solution to the cluster analysis above, it is immediately noticeable that all of the countries on the left-hand side of the Ward.D clustering are higher democracy countries. Of these, New Zealand and Canada were deviant for coverage so did not appear in the fsQCA solution, and so the clustering positions of these two countries are a closer fit in relation to the outcome measure. This positioning in relation to the outcome measure continues in relation to Belgium and the USA, which appear separate from the countries with higher democracy solutions, but were cases deviant for coverage in the QCA sufficient solution.

The complete linkage clustering solution, as it clusters the countries at a higher level in a different way to Ward.D, does not split the countries as obviously into countries with higher and lower set membership scores. Even so, many of the clusters between higher democracy countries remain in place at the lower level. If we take the right-hand fork of the dendrogram, all the countries located there are higher democracy countries (the Netherlands, Sweden, Switzerland, Ireland, Iceland, Norway, Denmark and Finland). At the top-level fork on the left-hand side, none of the countries is in the higher democracy set (Belgium, Israel, Greece, Italy, Japan, Korea, the UK and the USA). In between those clusters, however, are a range of countries, some of which are higher democracy (Australia, Canada and New Zealand, but with New Zealand and Canada deviant for coverage in the QCA solution), and with the remainder, which are positioned closest to one another, not in the higher set of democratic countries.

As such, there does seem to be overlap between the cluster analysis and the QCA solutions, even if we have to work a little harder to see it than we did in Chapter 3. The dendrograms, with a little digging, do seem to reveal key clusters of countries in terms of their democratic performance.

## DISCUSSION

The QCA necessary conditions in this chapter, those of lower levels of income inequality or higher levels of GDP, appear not as alternatives but as complements in the most important sufficient solutions for higher levels of democracy. These two factors form the root of solutions and a clear imperative: that, as countries grow richer, if they are to also have higher levels of democracy, they need to carefully consider issues of redistribution. It is possible, as Australia shows, to have higher levels of income inequality and still achieve democracy, and so there is a small degree of equifinality in the sufficient solution, but overwhelmingly countries with higher democratic ratings are richer, but also have lower levels of income inequality. These two factors appear to fit together.

Alongside the importance of higher income and lower income inequality, three of the four pathways also include higher levels of tertiary solution participation in their solution term. In the 21st century, there has been a significant expansion in higher education often justified in terms of raising skill levels, but expanding higher education also seems to lead to a higher democracy score as well. As economies, post-COVID, look like entering into periods of retrenchment where funding for higher education might be cut, policymakers need to be aware that this could affect the skill base and the democratic life of the country, and so have far-reaching consequences. This appears to stand in contrast to Frank's findings that the increased stress on higher education in the USA has served to divide the Democratic party, but it also emphasizes the importance of considering causal factors in conjunctions, and especially in relation to levels of income inequality.

As well as these three factors (higher income per capita, lower inequality and higher tertiary education participation), a factor that has been highlighted in previous chapters as important also appears in three of the four sufficient solution pathways – that of highly integrative government. This again makes sense in the context of the other factors: for democracy to be effective, there need to be opportunities for different interests to be able to make their case and participate in governmental processes. As noted earlier in the chapter, some theorists have advocated taking a more 'sortition' based approach to democracy in which we might elect our officials by chance to try to deal with disturbing findings about the levels of political education in our countries. The findings from this chapter may or may not conflict with that view. Highly integrative government would seek to incorporate a range of interests, but if elected agents can represent the people of their country more generally, then sortition becomes less necessary. It remains a question, however, as to how well our political representatives are currently listening to people with views different from their own.

Findings about the lack of political understanding from many people in our countries do remain deeply concerning. Perhaps that research, most of which has been generated from studies in the USA and UK, and which is not in the set of higher democracy countries, may not represent countries in the solution sets here, but democracy does depend on having an engaged and knowledgeable public, and clearly governments of all ideologies and backgrounds have a great deal to do in respect of this. This challenge is added to by the degree of false information being spread via internet platforms of different kinds. During the pandemic, falsehoods about vaccinations and the mechanisms of the spread of the virus have been a significant barrier to protecting many of the most vulnerable. It is hard to see how this propagation of falsehood without consequence can be allowed to continue.

Globalization was included as a key causal factor, and higher levels of globalization appear in the first and fourth solution pathways. This finding, which covers most of the countries in the solution set, points to globalization, in itself, as representing neither a pro- nor an anti-democratic force, but as a factor that can be managed, when combined with the other causal factors in the solution term. Globalization does not have to lead to a low-skill, low-pay economy – many of the countries in this solution term have found a different way that appears to lead to rather better outcomes for their people.

The results section also highlighted countries that are particularly interesting for a range of reasons.

First, Finland and Australia appear in the QCA solution, but effectively as individual pathways of their own (Australia appears with the USA, but the USA is deviant for consistency). Australia is a higher national income, higher education country, but has, in contrast to most of the solution pathways, higher levels of income inequality, lower levels of globalization and lower integrative government. This pattern works for Australia being a higher democracy nation, but does lead to the same outcome for the USA. It seems that, as it was in relation to preventable mortality, Australia represents a unique example rather than a template for others to follow. Australia's democracy is a relatively new one, and scores highly on electoral process (with a compulsory voting system), the functioning of its government and on its political culture.

Finland is a distinctive equifinal solution to achieving higher democracy, again showing the importance of taking a conjunctive approach to exploring solutions rather than one-size-fits-all. Finland scores well in all the dimensions present in the Economist measures of democracy, and especially well in terms of its electoral process and political participation. It seems that Finns have plenty of routes for engaging with political life. This fits with the country's measure of higher integrative government and lower income inequality, and might be seen as counterbalancing its lower tertiary education and lower national income.

As well as the countries that are unusual in the sufficient solution, there are also two cases that are deviant for consistency, and two that are deviant for coverage. Belgium and the USA are deviant for consistency, so have patterns of causal factors generally associated with strong democracy scores, but those countries do not achieve them. Both countries, it is fair to say, have had their own versions of democratic crisis in the last few years.

Belgium has struggled to achieve a stable government in the last few years, with its government being shut down for extended periods because of the lack of ability of its political parties to form a coalition. Belgium appears to be increasingly struggling to find common ground between the representatives of different cultural groups (Debeuf 2020). It has an integrative government structure, but is increasingly unable to bring the groups it needs together to form effective government. In the Economist Index, Belgium is described as a 'flawed democracy' not because of its electoral process, but because of its very low political participation and political culture scores, which seem to result from the challenges it is facing. These challenges have to be a source of concern for Belgians, but also for the European Union because of the centrality of Belgium to that enterprise.

The USA has also been through a period of considerable instability. Its political parties appear to be increasingly partisan (Achen and Bartels 2016), and the presidential elections of 2016 and 2020 made visible cracks in electoral processes (around the link between the public vote and electoral votes) clearly showing that changes to that process are needed. On 6 January 2021 the Capitol building was invaded by protesters, apparently fuelled by comments from President Trump around the election being unfair. Although the USA has many advantages in terms of its causal factors, and portrays itself as a beacon of freedom and democracy for the rest of the world, it appears to have significant struggles ahead of it, with legislation being considered to require additional identity documents before voting (something that also appears in the UK), which could suppress voting for a range of minority groups as a result. The United States is also labelled by the Economist as a flawed democracy, with its functionings of government rating, as measured during the Trump administration, being its lowest.

In terms of cases deviant for coverage, New Zealand and Canada achieve higher democracy scores despite not fitting with the QCA sufficient causal solutions. New Zealand appears on the same truth table row as Greece, with lower tertiary education, higher income inequality, lower globalization, lower integrative government and lower income per capita. Except perhaps for lower globalization, all these factors appear to point to New Zealand not having a higher democracy score.

It has certainly been the case that New Zealand, under the leadership of Jacinda Ardern, has been amongst the most successful countries in the world in dealing with COVID-19. New Zealand put in place hard borders early in the pandemic, and so successfully prevented transmission of the virus into the country. When we see coverage of New Zealand sport or cultural events, it can seem, to the rest of the world, that life is going on as normal.

New Zealand went through a process of electoral reform in the 1990s, moving away from the first-past-the-post system to a mixed member proportional representation system, which New Zealanders voted for overwhelmingly in a national referendum. New Zealand is one of the countries to score a full ten for its electoral process. Although it has a formal structure of political interests based around political parties, it has amongst the most transparent governments in the world, and has one of the lowest levels of political corruption. New Zealand appears to be as successful as a democracy because of these two factors (high honesty, low corruption), as well as its ability to govern locally in a more inclusive way, especially in more collaborative modes of governance with its Maori peoples.

Canada appears on the same truth table row as Spain and the UK, as having higher tertiary education, higher income inequality, higher globalization, but lower integrative government and lower levels of national income per capita. In the context of this combination of causal factors, Canada is achieving a stronger democracy score than we would expect – but with its higher income inequality and lower integrative government acting against the functioning of its democracy. There is some evidence for this, with Canada's political participation score being its lowest in the Economist index. However, Canada's functioning of government is significantly higher than that for Spain or the UK, as is its political culture score, suggesting that, although there are causal factors that might be a cause of concern, it is not struggling with quite the same degree of challenges as found in Spain and the UK. However, given it has the same causal factors as those two countries, there are surely dangers for Canada and it might regard those two countries as offering a warning as to how things could deteriorate.

The relationship between the cluster diagrams and the QCA solutions was stronger than in Chapter 5, but not as strong as in Chapter 3. We can clearly see the dendrogram being linked to the QCA solutions, but also some disagreement between the clustering linkage methods about the overall structure of the data. The smaller degree of equifinality present in the QCA solutions appears to help explain this.

Finally, it is also the case that three countries that have performed strongly in previous chapters do so again in this one – those of Norway, Sweden and Iceland. These three countries appear to have causal factors that consistently link to stronger performance in relation to the New Giants.

## CONCLUSION

This chapter presented the findings for causal conditions connected to achieve a higher score on the Economist Democracy Index, chosen as it most accurately captured the dimensions of democratic governance and participation that were identified as being of greatest concern as a New Giant.

The necessary conditions for a higher democracy score, higher GDP or lower income inequality, were logical alternatives, but in fact combined in most of the countries in the sufficient solution, with lower income inequality and higher GDP per capita. For the majority of the countries in the sufficient solution, these two factors also combined with higher tertiary education participation to form a combination of factors that appear to support stronger democracies. In addition to these three terms, countries either have higher globalization or higher integrative government, with the latter being a more obvious theoretical fit, and so perhaps forming an ideal-type template of causal factors. Higher globalization remains a more contentious inclusion, but it is important that many of the countries achieving higher democracy scores are also highly globalized, suggesting that significant globalization can at least be accommodated by other causal factors, or at best be part of a supportive combination of factors that are linked to highly democratic nations.

It is clear from the review above, as well as from the Economist Democracy Index, that democratic governance is more fragile than we would like. Politicians from both the UK and USA appear to be calling for measures that might restrict elections to citizens more prepared to engage with identity checks, claiming that this would prevent voter fraud, but there seems precious little evidence of such fraud. This appears to suggest that such measures are perhaps more about restricting voting, and this cannot lead to a better functioning democratic state. The inclusion of integrative government in one of the two main solution pathways appears to suggest that the more we incorporate different interests into governance, the stronger our democracies become. However, it also incumbent on politicians to work together to find solutions, with Belgium and the USA case studies of what can happen when those processes break down.

There was a small degree of equifinality in the sufficient solution pathways, with Australia and Finland presenting different routes to a strong democracy, but these appear to be less templates for others to follow than as reminders that there are a number of different ways of achieving highly functioning democracies. That these countries are picked up by QCA shows the importance of both conjunctional causation and equifinality in that method.

The next chapter considers job quality as the fourth of the New Giants.

## NOTE

1.   Available at http://www.eiu.com/topic/democracy-index/ (accessed on 11 November 2021).

# 7. Job quality

## INTRODUCTION

In 1942 Beveridge made the assumption that, in the post-war period, full employment would be the norm (in practice, he meant unemployment below 8.5%). In the aftermath of the mass unemployment of the 1930s, this was extraordinary and, even in the face of the uncertainty of what would follow World War 2, it showed a considerable optimism about the future. What were the reasons for this optimism?

Although the 1930s are best known economically for being a period of economic depression, they were also a time of considerable innovation in economic theory and governance. In terms of theory, Keynes published his *General Theory of Employment, Interest and Money* in 1936 (Keynes 1997), which systematized the view that the government should play an active role in macroeconomic management, especially through fiscal policy. It should do this by increasing spending and 'pump-priming' the economy during periods of economic slowdown, and reducing its expenditures in periods of boom, and so effectively regulating the business cycle. Keynes provided a series of intellectual justifications for greater government intervention than had been the case before the 1930s, legitimizing governments running deficits in recessions to help the economy recover from them, so long as they then ran surpluses in times of boom to slow down excessive growth. The former was adopted by governments with enthusiasm, but the latter proved more difficult to achieve.

In terms of economic governance, the US President Franklin D. Roosevelt had experimented with his 'New Deal' in the 1930s, acting against economic orthodoxy and extending the role of government support during the Great Depression. Furious debate surrounds the effects of his actions, and whether they improved the US Economy, but perhaps most importantly they broke new ground and showed that governments could adopt a more interventionist stance.

Beveridge's first assumption was that the economy could be managed to achieve full employment. This assumption, in turn, rested upon a second one, that of a relatively closed national economy. For macroeconomic demand management to work, a government has to be able to control both fiscal and monetary flows inside of its domain. If there are large financial flows in and out of an economy, then this can quickly destabilize government plans.

Beveridge's third assumption was about the nature of employment. Although Beveridge was an expert in the area of employment, and having been instrumental in setting up 'Labour Exchanges' (what we might now term 'Job Centres'), his view of employment would have been concerned with full-time workers who were predominantly male. Looking wider, most of those jobs would have been in manufacturing, with this period coming to be known as 'Fordism', or the mass production of consumer goods.

All three of Beveridge's assumptions have now been critically undermined. Keynesian demand management remains with us, but without any commitment from the government to secure full employment. Globalization has led to assumptions about closed national economies no longer being sustainable, especially given the massive financial flows that can occur in an instant, and the rise of multinational corporations that can locate their bases wherever they wish. What is meant by 'full employment' has changed dramatically, with the growth of part-time work, but also the 'gig economy' in which contracts are often limited to specific tasks with little or no long-term commitment (or benefits) from employers. Assumptions about men forming the majority of the labour market have not been sustainable for decades, even if the long road to labour market equality still has a way to go. Finally, the mass production of Fordism has given way to flexible production strategies, a much smaller manufacturing sector, and a rise in service sector work that is often (in the UK and USA) far less unionized, and so has far fewer 'countervailing' forces (Galbraith 1975) in employment relations.

All these factors have combined to change the world considerably. Governments have, on the one hand, made commitments to raising skill levels in their economies to try to ensure that productivity levels can rise, and to try to ensure an educated and capable labour force is available (Jessop 2002). Investment in tertiary education has risen. At the same time, however, labour markets in many countries have become less regulated, a move justified on the grounds that global competitive forces require both workers and firms to be more 'agile' or 'flexible' in response. This seems to have led to a range of different state strategies being possible, with mixes of 'flexicurity' (high-skill, high-pay workers working flexibly on their own terms) and 'flexploitation' (lower skill, low-pay workers on more precarious contracts) (Viebrock and Clasen 2009).

Ground-breaking work from Thelen (2014) explores many of these issues in a comparative study of the United States, Germany, Denmark, Sweden and the Netherlands, showing the complex relationship between increasing labour market flexibility and the quality of work. 'Flexibility' is often presented as a pejorative term, synonymous with exploitation, but Thelen reminds us that flexibility can be of benefit to all types of workers, and act as a means of improving job quality, provided it occurs in a context in which there are strong opportunities for education and training in an economy, and where governmental strategies based on competing on a global scale through low-cost labour are avoided.

The 2020s are also a time of increased automation. This dates back to the 1960s and 1970s in large-scale industrial production, with the introduction of robots that could repeat small tasks endlessly. However, as computer processing power increases and more roles can be described through the development of new algorithms, increasingly skilled work is being replaced by computers. It appears that such computers still require supervision by skilled workers, but there is a clear sense of threat to work being increasingly replaced as these new expert systems become more sophisticated.

In the face of these changes, there have been calls for the introduction of a 'basic' or 'universal' income (Painter and Thoung 2015). The idea here is to reallocate welfare spending across a range of benefits to give everyone in an economy a guaranteed payment each month. As more people find themselves on low incomes, and so in weaker and weaker bargaining positions, such a basic income would give them back the ability to choose to work or not, as well as fostering a stronger sense of 'belonging' through the receipt of that income. Advocates point to experiments showing that such a payment is viable and has positive results (Millar 2009). However, no developed country has gone fully down this road yet, and so it cannot form the basis of the comparison here.

What we can do is explore a range of factors which appear relevant to job quality, and find an outcome measure that differentiates between countries to explore which have managed to maintain job quality despite the pressures outlined above, and what they have in common.

## CAUSAL FACTORS

The factors considered in this chapter are as follows:

First, given the importance of processes around globalization in the discussion above, including a measure of this factor is clearly important. The book has included the KOF Globalization measure already, and given its coverage of financial flows, trade flows, as well as more cultural measures of globalization, including it here as well appears a good choice, allowing cross-chapter comparison with chapters 4 and 6, where it also appears as a causal factor. The question, here, is whether countries with higher levels of measured globalization also have measures of lower job quality.

The second and third causal factors included in this chapter consider the extent to which government is attempting to pursue (or not) a low-cost labour market strategy, which, as we saw above, is more likely to lead to a strategy of 'flexploitation' rather than 'flexicurity'. To consider this, the first factor we incorporate is that of the level of public social expenditure. Public social expenditure is clearly not solely about the labour market, but it gives an index of a societal commitment to confronting market imperfections and supporting people through the use of public funds. It gives us, to use Esping-Andersen's (1990) terms, at least some idea of the degree of 'decommodification' present in a society, or the extent of commitment to the non-market economy. Exploring the relationship between public social expenditure and job quality is important as it can consider competing points on the debate concerning whether higher social spending is there to 'prop up' low job quality, or is likely to indicate a higher skill economy because of the higher levels of taxation it might imply.

As well as including public social expenditure, it is also useful to consider the extent of inequality within a society. As a starting point, we might suspect that higher levels of inequality might be linked to lower levels of job quality (at least for a significant proportion of people) and the labour market being split, as suggested above, into groups who benefit from those arrangements, and large numbers of people who are less skilled not experiencing the same rise in standards of living. As with other chapters, the GINI measure (post transfers) gives at least some insight into this, as well as making the research in the book compatible with other studies that incorporate this widely used measure.

The final two factors are those included in all other chapters of the book. First, there is Maleki and Hendriks's 'integrative government' measure, from which we might have good grounds of expecting more integrative governments to also be those with higher job quality. The causal link here is through wider societal representation in government leading to a rejection of aiming for a strategy of trying to achieve a low cost rather than high skill workforce. Considering this factor allows us to see, in relation to other factors, whether this is the case or not.

Finally, the book's other consistent measure is that of tertiary education participation. The inclusion of this question aims to deal with a simple question: do higher levels of tertiary education lead to economies with higher job quality? Government policy over the last thirty years has been based around the building of higher levels of skills through the expansion of higher education. What has this led to in terms of job quality?

From these causal factors, we can put in place directional (theoretical) expectations, which suggest that higher levels of tertiary education, lower levels of income inequality and higher levels of public social expenditure might be causally linked to higher levels of job quality. As such, counterfactuals including these factors will be included in the calculation of the intermediate sufficient solution presented above. As in other chapters, however, those assumptions will not be in place in the calculation of the conservative or parsimonious sufficient solutions, however, which can then be contrasted with these expectations (as with the solution terms themselves).

Finding an outcome measure that allows comparison of the countries included here for job quality is challenging. Although there are recent measures of job quality, they tend to be for a limited range of countries only. The best I have been able to find is the OECD measure, which is based on three further measures from the OECD's own database. These measures are earnings quality, labour market security, and quality of the working environment. Earnings quality measures earnings in relation to average earnings as well as how they are distributed across the workforce. Labour market insecurity is concerned with the risk of unemployment and, where people are unemployed, the levels of benefit they receive. The quality of the working environment considers the nature and content of work in terms of the demands put on workers, and the resources workers have to deal with those demands. These are all technical measures in themselves, and are aggregated to produce the overall job quality index.

However, because of the complexity of the calculations underlying the job quality index, the measures are not as frequently updated as they are for more straightforward numbers reported by the OECD. This is frustrating, but there is an absence of alternative measures for all the countries in the dataset here. Up-to-date measures for earnings quality and labour market insecurity are available, but not for the quality of the working environment ('job strain').

To consider these measures further a principal components analysis was conducted to see if they could be combined into a single measure. The first principal component, however, would account for only around 65% of the variance of the two variables. That meant a choice of outcome measure between the variables was needed. After performing analysis with both variables, the measure of earnings quality appeared to have the highest validity in terms of the rank order of the countries it produced. Taking labour market insecurity instead graded countries such as Sweden and Denmark as being amongst those in the set of poor job quality, and existing research would question a distribution based around that claim (Thelen 2014). The alternative was to specifically calibrate to include countries that research indicates have lower levels of insecurity, but this would have resulted in a highly skewed dataset, and therefore achieving little in terms of comparison. The earnings quality measure, in contrast, appeared to produce a more balanced calibration which tied to existing research. It was therefore included as the outcome measure here.

Having 2010 only outcome measures in place also presented another dilemma: most of the causal factors included here have measures from 2019. In order to explore what difference it made using data from 2009 instead, all the datasets were recalculated using data from that year, but with calibrations coming out at very similar levels. I therefore decided to retain the 2019 figures for causal factors in the book's analysis in order to keep the data directly comparable with other chapters in the book, despite the odd logic this leads to (combining 2019 causal factors with a 2010 outcome measure). However, the gain here is in presenting a simpler overall dataset, more consistent cross-chapter comparisons, and with very little difference in reported solutions from using data from the earlier period.

## CLUSTER ANALYSIS

The cluster analysis data included here was produced with the causal factors outlined in the previous section, and attempted to add additional weight to the outcome measure by also including the OECD labour market insecurity index (which is included alongside job quality in the OECD's series) to explore whether countries clustered on both of these factors (r=-0.265, p.006).

The Ward linkage method of clustering produced the result below.

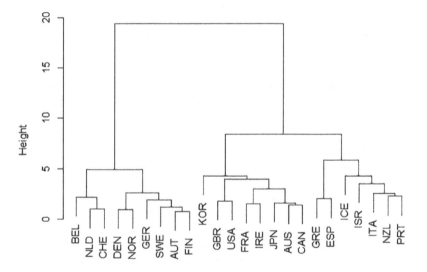

*Figure 7.1      Ward linkage – job quality*

Working from the top of the dendrogram downwards, Ward.D clustering produces two distinct clusters of countries positioned towards the left- and right-hand sides of the dendrogram. On the left are Western European countries, a clustering that is familiar from previous chapters, but also with some exceptions. The UK is clustered closely with the USA on the right-hand side of the diagram, where France and Ireland are also clustered together. The right-hand side is more mixed geographically, but with clusters of southern Europe (Greece, Spain, Portugal and Italy), and also with Australia, Canada and Japan close to one another, as are Iceland and Israel.

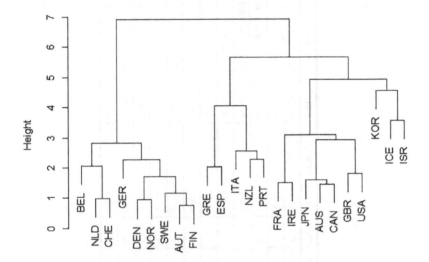

*Figure 7.2    Complete linkage – job quality*

Complete clustering produces a slightly different ordering, but otherwise identical in terms of the two main clusterings in the dendrogram. This appears to suggest that there is, at least at the top level, a strong degree of consistency in terms of the countries' positions in relation to one another based on these data. The next section outlines the QCA results before they are combined with the cluster analysis.

## QCA RESULTS

If we move on to the first stage of fsQCA, and the search for necessary conditions, the combination of either higher integrative government or higher public social expenditure has a consistency of 0.911 and a relevance of 0.76, as well as having a strong theoretical underpinning. Higher integrative government should include a range of interests and incorporate their views in policymaking, and in the context of job quality this would suggest that there is the potential for organized labour representation to have a strong chance of being included in government. Higher levels of public social expenditure

*Table 7.1*    Table truth – job quality

| MHINT | PUBSOCEXP | EDUCTERT | GINIPOST | KOFGLOB19 | OUT | CONSISTENCY | PRI | CASES |
|---|---|---|---|---|---|---|---|---|
| 0 | 0 | 0 | 1 | 0 | 0 | 0.639 | 0.021 | GRE, NZL |
| 0 | 0 | 0 | 1 | 1 | 0 | 0.703 | 0.145 | PRT |
| 0 | 0 | 1 | 1 | 0 | 0 | 0.706 | 0.230 | AUS, JPN, KOR |
| 0 | 0 | 1 | 1 | 1 | 0 | 0.795 | 0.199 | CAN, ESP, GBR |
| 0 | 1 | 1 | 0 | 1 | 1 | 0.914 | 0.730 | FRA, IRE |
| 0 | 1 | 1 | 1 | 0 | 0 | 0.870 | 0.125 | USA |
| 1 | 0 | 1 | 0 | 0 | 0 | 0.934 | 0.607 | ICE |
| 1 | 0 | 1 | 0 | 1 | 1 | 0.960 | 0.902 | NLD |
| 1 | 0 | 1 | 1 | 0 | 0 | 0.736 | 0.065 | ISR |
| 1 | 1 | 0 | 0 | 1 | 1 | 0.949 | 0.903 | AUT, FIN, GER |
| 1 | 1 | 0 | 1 | 0 | 0 | 0.888 | 0.190 | ITA |
| 1 | 1 | 1 | 0 | 1 | 1 | 0.959 | 0.928 | BEL, DEN, NOR, SWE, CHE |

suggest a government committed to wider social goals, and job quality might be amongst those.

The next stage of fsQCA is the construction of a truth table, which can be seen in Table 7.1. This truth table has several rows that exhibit combinations of factors with high consistency scores but low PRI scores, indicating possible instances of simultaneous subset relations – of combinations that appear to fit with both the higher and lower job quality solutions. This applies to the row with Canada, Spain and the UK, which falls just below the 0.8 consistency threshold, but has a low PRI score (0.199), and most clearly to the rows with the USA and Italy, which despite their high consistency scores (0.870 and 0.888 respectively), have very low PRI scores. All of these countries were reviewed because of the possibility of having simultaneous subset relations, and so appearing in both the solution for higher and lower job quality, and on that basis were excluded from the calculation for the sufficient solution for higher job quality.

The intermediate sufficient solution requires the setting of directional expectations. Here expectations of higher public social expenditure, higher tertiary education and lower income inequality were set. Higher public social expenditure was a necessary condition as well as having a strong theoretical fit, but we would also expect higher levels of tertiary education to be present in economies with higher skills; and the more people with such skills, the higher the availability of good-quality jobs. Lower income inequality would be suggestive of high job quality being more widely available than for an elite group of workers alone.

The intermediate sufficient solution is presented in Table 7.2, and was identical to the conservative one, suggesting the chosen directional expectations had limited impact in this case.

*Table 7.2    Sufficient intermediate solution – job quality*

| Solution | Consistency | PRI | Coverage | Unique coverage | Cases |
|---|---|---|---|---|---|
| MHINT* ~GINI | 0.953 | 0.924 | 0.612 | 0.212 | ICE, NLD AUT, FIN, GER, BEL, DEN, NOR, SWE, CHE |
| PUBSO CEXP*E DUCTER T*~GINI* KOFGLOB | 0.926 | 0.870 | 0.461 | 0.061 | FRA, IRE, BEL, DEN, NOR, SWE, CHE |

120 *Welfare states in the 21st century*

The intermediate sufficient solution had a consistency of 0.931, and a coverage of 0.673. The solution here presents two pathways only, and with some degree of overlap between the two.

The first pathway combines highly integrative government with lower income inequality. It covers ten countries (Iceland, the Netherlands, Austria, Finland, Germany, Belgium, Denmark, Norway, Sweden and Switzerland), with no countries deviant for consistency, suggesting this is a robust solution pathway to high earnings quality. This pathway also has the highest unique coverage in the solution term, so is empirically the most important.

The second pathway combines higher public social expenditure and higher tertiary education with lower income inequality (in common with the first solution pathway) and higher globalization, bringing France and Ireland into the solution (instead of Austria and the Netherlands in pathway one), but alongside Belgium, Denmark, Norway, Sweden and Switzerland from the first pathway. However, Ireland is a case deviant for consistency.

There are two countries deviant for coverage in the solution – Australia and Canada.

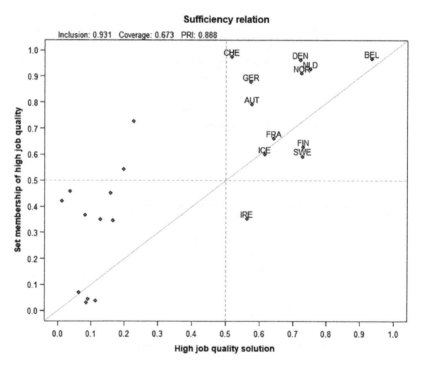

*Figure 7.3*  *Sufficient solution – job quality*

The cases can be visualized by plotting the solution against the set membership, which appears as follows, and which shows that IRE is a relatively marginal case in terms of being deviant for consistency.

## COMPARISON OF CLUSTER ANALYSIS WITH QCA SOLUTION

If we move on to considering our cluster analysis in relation to the sufficient solution, then a very strong relationship between the two appears.

On the Ward.D clustering, the left-hand side of the dendrogram contains Belgium, the Netherlands, Switzerland, Denmark, Norway, Germany, Sweden, Austria and Finland. These nine countries all appear in the QCA solution term for high earnings quality. However, this clustering of countries misses out France, Iceland and Ireland that were present in the QCA solution (albeit with the latter deviant for consistency). It also omits Australia and Canada, which have high earnings quality but were deviant for coverage in the QCA solution.

The complete linkage method gives an almost identical result, suggesting that different clustering methods here make little difference, and also, given the fairly strong fit with the sufficient QCA results, that the solution is one that is robust from different analytical perspectives. The cluster analysis therefore gives a clear steer as to the countries with high earnings quality, but with some notable exceptions appearing outside of the main clustering of countries sharing that outcome.

## DISCUSSION

The two pathways to higher job quality have only one causal factor in common, but overlap in terms of the countries that they cover. Lower levels of income inequality appear in both solution pathways, and appear to confirm that idea that job quality, if it is not to be available to an elite group only, needs an economy and society that is prepared to be more redistributive.

The first solution pathway links highly integrative government with lower income inequality, suggesting that countries able to bring wider interests into government are more likely to be concerned with achieving better job quality. This combination of factors is highly consistent in the solution, and makes a great deal of theoretical sense.

The second solution pathway is more complex. It has lower income inequality, but combines it with higher tertiary education participation, higher social expenditure and higher globalization. Once again, higher globalization appears as part of a sufficient solution when we may have been concerned that a highly globalized economy might also reduce job quality. However, provided there is also a concern with keeping income inequality lower, and having a highly skilled workforce, as well as emphasizing the redistributionary nature of the economy and society through higher levels of public social expenditure, this does not have to be the case.

There is one case deviant for consistency in the QCA solution, with Ireland having a mix of causal factors associated with higher job quality, but not achieving a score at that level. Ireland appears on the same truth table row as France, and in the second solution pathway, which combines higher public social expenditure with higher tertiary education, lower income inequality and higher globalization. Why, then, does this not seem to work for Ireland when it does for the other six countries with this pattern of causal factors?

The 2012 Eurofound study on job quality in Europe (Eurofound 2012) found that Ireland has one of the highest proportions of high-quality jobs in Europe, but also above-average numbers of people with *lower* job quality. Ireland has increased the skill level of its people, but also has above-average levels of jobs at risk, and amongst the lowest overall ratings for prospects for workers. All of these factors appear to point to a segregated labour market. Part of this is the significant presence of international companies in Ireland, who often employ highly skilled workers and are linked to its higher globalization rating. On the other hand, Ireland often appears to struggle in terms of job quality in more traditional areas (often labelled as 'indigenous') based around agriculture, travel and tourism. Ireland, then, faces considerable challenges in 'balancing' job quality across these groups, and may also be at substantial risk should its international companies decide to relocate.

There are two cases deviant for coverage – countries that do not appear in the QCA sufficient solution, despite having high job quality – and they are Australia and Canada.

Australia, as I have outlined in previous chapters of the book, falls consistently outside QCA solutions, but still manages to achieve strong outcomes. Australia appears on the same truth table row as Japan and Korea, neither of which has high job quality. Australia's success appears to rest on its having both a very high employment rate, combined with a low unemployment rate (OECD 2018). These factors, combined with low labour market insecurity, allow workers who lose their jobs to find new employment relatively straightforwardly. A great deal of Australia's success then, appears to rest on its dynamic labour market, coupled with consistent economic growth, with its traditional industries, especially mining, continuing to play a significant role in this. As such, Australia appears to overcome the challenges of some of its causal factors, especially higher-income inequality and lower levels of public social expenditure, by having such a vibrant labour market. There are questions, though, about the long-term viability of traditional industries such as mining, as well as of the gap in job quality between its white and indigenous peoples.

Canada appears on the same truth table row as Spain and the UK, with higher levels of income inequality and lower public social expenditure (factors that are also shared with Australia), as well as higher levels of globalization. A first review of the data reveals that Canada lies just inside the set of countries with high job quality (with a fuzzy-set score of 0.54), so is a marginal case. In the context of OECD data, Canada has above-average earnings quality, and below-average labour market insecurity. In-depth research (Chen et al. 2018) suggests that Canada does face a range of challenges; the labour market becoming segmented in terms of job quality on socio-demographic lines, and with some of the largest hospitality and personal service sectors having low job quality across multiple dimensions. Although Canada's more flexible job market appears to have been an asset in the past, the authors suggest that it could now stand 'in the way of inclusive growth and a robust economy' (p.28). As such, although Canada is a case deviant for coverage, it only just falls into the set of countries with high job quality, and is facing significant challenges, and so does not perhaps offer a template for other countries to follow.

Finally, attentive readers will have noticed that the three countries that have been most able to address the New Giants – Norway, Sweden and Iceland – were also present in the sufficient solutions in this chapter as well. As we move to the fifth New Giant, those countries appear to be the ones that are most consistently addressing the global challenges we face in the 21st century.

## CONCLUSION

This chapter presented both cluster analysis and QCA solutions in relation to job quality. The two different approaches appear to converge strongly, with there being only two, highly consistent QCA solution pathways.

High job quality appears through two different routes, but these overlap. One pathway is based on highly integrative governments and lower income inequality, both of which are credible causal factors in terms of the literature review in this chapter, and present economies that appear to include a wide variety of interests, and aim to achieve job quality across all of them.

The second pathway is a combination of higher public social expenditure, higher tertiary education, lower income inequality and higher globalization. The first three factors here fit together coherently, and perhaps offer a buffer to any of the worst effects of globalization. It is also important to stress that the two pathways overlap in terms of countries, with Belgium, Denmark, Norway, Sweden and Switzerland appearing in both – and so having a combination of all of these factors. This combination of causal factors might then be regarded as an ideal type template, combining highly integrative government that aims for lower income inequality, higher public social expenditure as a means of redistribution as well as providing strong public services, and higher tertiary education participation to aim for a highly skilled workforce, which is able to compete in the global economy.

There are countries that do not have this pattern of factors, and yet still have high job quality, and we discussed the cases of Australia and Canada in that light. We also discussed the case of Ireland, which, because of its highly polarized job market, does not achieve high job quality despite fitting with one of the solution pathways.

The next chapter moves on to the last of the New Giants, that of environmental degradation.

# 8.   Environmental degradation

## INTRODUCTION

If there is one new challenge that captures the ethos of the New Giants most clearly, it is that of environmental degradation. This is truly global in scope, and the result of unintended actions by billions of humans over several decades. Individual governments, even the largest ones, appear to be struggling to confront it (or even, in some cases, to accept that climate change is the result of human action, and is happening). Climate change is such an overwhelming problem that many of us do our best to put it out of our minds, categorizing it as too difficult to deal with, or so vast in scope that there is little we can do about it.

However, climate change is an existential threat to our future. If we persist in our present behaviours, there will be calamitous effects upon billions of people across the world. Even within the scope of my own lifetime, changes to the patterns of weather are clear. Extreme weather events are becoming more common across the world, and temperatures are rising. While it is true that we are often caught up in other challenges (as I write this, the COVID-19 pandemic), climate change remains a constant threat requiring global co-ordinated action to deal with. Meetings of our leaders have resulted in some promises of action (and some leaders refusing to participate at all), but unless we do things differently, and learn from countries that are already making progress, we risk destroying all our futures (and those that follow us) because of our lack of ability to act.

One of the key theorists whose work this book has engaged with is Anthony Giddens. Giddens's book *The Politics of Climate Change* (2011) brings together the challenges involved in environmental degradation, making clear in its introduction that it is our everyday behaviour and daily routines that contribute to climate change, and of the difficulty of facing up to the changes needed even though much of the science is generally accepted by credible people in the field. Giddens presents a paradox, which he names after himself, and which states that, since the dangers posed by global warming aren't tangible, in the sense of being visible in most of our daily lives, it is easier to do nothing about them. But waiting until climate problems become visible will probably mean we are acting too late.

Giddens suggest that this paradox affects almost every aspect of our current response to climate change; even though most of the public accept it as a threat, only a relative few would be prepared to fundamentally change their lives. This results in a great deal of gesture politics, and grand plans for the future (claims of aiming to be 'carbon neutral' by a date far from now), when action is needed today. There seems to a lack of collective will, or even a developed analysis of what is politically needed to confront climate change.

States are clearly key actors in confronting the New Giant of Environment Degradation. Despite the claims of the most ardent globalization theorists, states retain a great deal of power in terms of both domestic and international policy. However, we cannot force the leaders of countries to sign up to international agreements; and even if they do, we still depend on them taking the action they have promised. States will have to provide the investment to make sure that technological advances occur that can support a lower-carbon future. States will also have to try and co-ordinate the myriad of other actors in each country, ranging from multinational corporations that may be reluctant to change their practices, to industries that are heavy polluters but large employers, through to the rest of us, who may feel that any action we can take is on such a small scale that it will make little difference.

The green movement has been a significant force in trying to raise the profile of environmental degradation as a global issue, and in some countries has become a major electoral force, especially where proportional representation allows for involvement of non-traditional political parties. But environmentalism can also square with the ideologies of mainstream political movements. The root of one version of Conservatism is in the preservation of the past (hence 'Conserve') and with that a strong link to the countryside and its preservation. Left-wing political parties have often embraced versions of environmentalism and attempted to incorporate them into their political agendas.

One of the major political barriers we face is that politicians often have short-term time horizons. They need to be elected, and then to remain in power. This often involves needing the support of industries that may dislike proposals designed to reduce environmental harm. In a period of recession, political focus is likely to be more on re-establishing economic growth, with the environmental falling quickly in terms of the list of priorities. Any actions politicians take is likely to take years to have effect, and so they are effectively passing on the potential benefits of trying to look after the environment to their successors, while having to deal with the costs themselves. This requires politicians to adopt long-term time horizons, putting doing the right thing ahead of the political problems it may cause them, even when it is their political heirs that will benefit.

It is also true that the exact risks involved in climate change cannot be precisely measured. We can see long-term trends, and create complex models to try to establish what might happen next, but we can't be sure. Climate change represents a new risk, probably created by human activity, but we don't know exactly where the tipping points are at which point things become irreversible. Although much of the science is settled in being sure that climate change is occurring, exactly what *kinds* of change we are seeing, and *when* further changes might happen, are harder to predict. This gives space to prominent sceptics who argue that the science is not settled (while it may not be settled on exact timings, but the overall direction is very clear), and creates room for populist politicians who want to campaign directly to those who do not wish to change their lives, or whose employment might be threatened by environmental legislation.

A further political challenge is what Giddens calls the 'development imperative'. Most developing nations have contributed very little to climate change, but they must be given the chance to improve the lives of their people and continue to develop their economies. The need for developing countries to grow would appear to suggest that further environmental harm is inevitable – but if richer countries are prepared to reduce their impact, and share their technologies with developing countries, this need not be the case. However, it will require significant government action, as well as an extension of international agreements.

Preventing climate change also offers significant opportunities for businesses, charities and NGOs to make massive contributions, and perhaps also a lot of money. If we can come up with new technologies that reduce environmental damage, there are global markets available to sell into. Governments need to support research in this area more fully. Governments also need to configure their taxation regimes to support firms that are doing their best to prevent climate change, and penalize those that are not (Krugman 2009; Stiglitz 2003). It may well be that international agreements need to be put in place to co-ordinate this regulation.

The challenge before us in terms of climate change is formidable. However, it is clear that some governments are doing more than others, and some countries are successful across a range of environmental measures. The next section considers the range of causal factors and the outcome measure that will be used in this chapter.

## CAUSAL FACTORS

If we move on to consider the causal factors most relevant to contributing to climate change, it means a search, as in other chapters, for what the governments making most progress against climate change have in common. It would be possible to put together a comparison based on a range of causal factors that are specific to the environmental domain, such as carbon emissions and measures of the energy infrastructure. However, this book wants to ask questions at a higher level, considering how political and social factors contribute to confronting the New Giants. The causal factors are a mix of those from previous chapters, including the two that are common to all chapters in the book. They are as follows:

First, given the strong links in the academic literature between globalization and climate change, both of which represent new 'risks' (Beck 1992; Beck et al. 1994), it is worth exploring the relationship between the two. Are the countries with the highest levels of globalization more likely to be successful in tacking it, or less? There are plausible claims on both sides. It is possible to see globalization as being driven by financial motives in which economic growth is the most important goal, and progress in confronting climate change could be seen as potentially compromising that growth. Equally, however, nations with high degrees of globalization might also have a wider outlook, as well as seeing the economic potential for new technologies, and so wish to engage more strongly with climate change. Amongst the countries here, and taking our other causal factors into account, which appears to be the case? As with other chapters in the book, the KOF Globalization Index is used to try to capture the multidimensional aspects of globalization, and how they play out through both cluster analysis and the calculation of sufficient QCA solutions.

The second factor included here is that of income inequality. In this case, income inequality can be regarded as a proxy to measure the extent of commitment a country has to resolving social issues. If a country allows higher levels of income inequality (post taxes and transfers) to occur, we might hypothesize that it will be less committed to other social goals, including dealing with climate change. Examining the data will allow us to consider this hypothesis.

Third, and given the increasing public attention on climate change often led by younger people, there is a question as to whether countries with higher levels of democratic participation are also those that are most committed to dealing with climate change. To explore this, the second dimension proposed by Maleki and Hendriks, which attempts to capture democratic participation, will be utilized. Are countries with higher levels of measured democratic participation also those that appear to be most committed to tackling climate change?

The last two factors are those in common with the other chapters of the book. The first is Maleki and Hendriks' first dimension of democratic governance, that of the extent of integrative government. This factor presents an interesting question as to whether more integrative government, involving more interests and more political parties, leads to a stronger commitment to confronting climate change, or results in a lack of ability to secure an agreement in the face of the challenge that it offers. Which appears to be the case?

Finally, the last causal factor is that of tertiary education participation. Do higher levels of tertiary education result in a better understanding in a country of the need to act to prevent climate change? We might expect that a combination of greater democratic participation and a higher level of tertiary education might result in governments more willing to tackle climate change. Is this the case?

As with the other New Giants, it's necessary to find an outcome measure that captures whether countries are both acting to deal with climate change in their jurisdictions, as well as engaging in global attempts to deal with the climate. Several possible measures exist, but the one with the strongest fit to the way climate change is conceptualized here comes from the Yale Centre for Environmental Law and Policy, the 'EPI' (Environmental Performance Index[1]). The index is made up of two domains: Environmental Health (air quality, sanitation and drinking water, heavy metals and waste management) and Ecosystem Validity (biodiversity and habitat, ecosystem services, fisheries, climate change, pollution emissions, agriculture, water resources). The EPI reports on 32 performance indicators across 11 issue categories measured for 180 countries. It is both a gauge of how close countries are to environmental policy targets and an indicator of which countries are best at addressing the environmental challenges all nations face. It therefore appears well suited to treating climate change as a New Giant.

## CLUSTER ANALYSIS

Cluster analysis was performed on the causal factors and outcome measures listed above, along with the two components of the EPI, environment health and ecosystem validity, to help balance the numbers of causal factors and outcomes.

The Ward.D linkage produced the dendrogram seen in Figure 8.1. From this dendrogram, and reading from the top, there is, as with other chapters, a split between a group of Western European nations on the left-hand side, and a more mixed pattern on the right. The right-hand fork includes the UK, France, Spain and Ireland, so there is some mixing of geographies, but with those countries often being located separately from others in West Europe in previous chapters as well.

The complete linkage method produces the clustering seen in Figure 8.2.

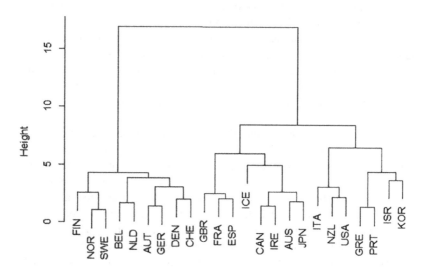

*Figure 8.1       Ward clustering – environment*

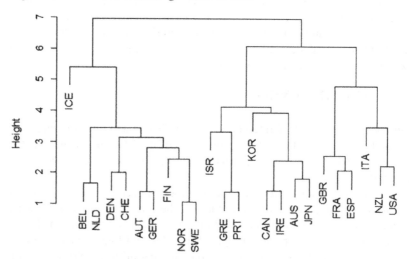

*Figure 8.2       Complete clustering – environment*

This dendrogram has a great deal in common with the Ward.D linkage dendro-gram, but ICE have moved from the right-hand side to the left, and there are some differences in ordering (especially around Korea and Israel). Otherwise, it seems there is a great deal in common between the results of the two linkage methods.

## QCA

The next stage of analysis is to move to fsQCA, and to consider necessary conditions.

When exploring the data, the factor with the highest relevance for a high EPI score was KOFGLOB (consistency 0.883, relevance 0.770), or highly globalized countries, and as there are, as we saw above, arguments for expecting highly globalized countries to also be more environmentally aware, this factor was included as necessary. A second possible factor, of highly integrative government with lower income inequality, also had a high consistency and relevance score (consistency 0.873, relevance 0.626) as well as being credible as a causal factor. As such, these two factors were included as being necessary in the calculation of the sufficient solutions below. However, when calculating the sufficient results, we found that the inclusion of exclusion of these factors did not affect the solutions that were generated.

The next stage in analysis is the calculation of the truth table which can be seen in Table 8.1.

There is one line of this truth table where the consistency threshold (0.8) was met, but the case was excluded from inclusion from the sufficient solution calculation because of its low PRI score, that of Iceland. This country's PRI score of 0.243 indicates a simultaneous subset relation, and so the case was excluded on this basis. It is also the case that New Zealand, with a consistency score of 0.794, and Australia and the USA, with consistency of 0.786, came very close to the consistency threshold, but were excluded, again on the basis of low PRI scores (0.111 and 0.203 respectively).

The intermediate sufficient QCA solution was calculated with directional expectations of highly integrative government and lower income inequality, with the view that more integrative government was more likely to have included the views of those seeking to preserve the environment, and lower levels of income inequality might suggest governments more concerned with curbing some of the excesses of consumerism. However, in practice, these directional expectations made little difference to the results.

The intermediate sufficient solution had three pathways and can be seen in Table 8.2.

The first solution pathway is a combination of lower integrative government (against theoretical expectations), higher tertiary education and higher globalization. It covers five countries, but with two (Ireland and Canada) deviant for consistency. As such, although this solution has the second-highest coverage, it has the lowest consistency of the three pathways.

Table 8.1     *Truth table – environment*

| MHINT | MHPART | EDUCTERT | KOFGLOB | GINIPOST | OUT | CONSISTENCY | PRI | CASES |
|---|---|---|---|---|---|---|---|---|
| 0 | 0 | 0 | 0 | 1 | 0 | 0.671 | 0.074 | GRE |
| 0 | 0 | 0 | 1 | 1 | 0 | 0.759 | 0.256 | PRT |
| 0 | 0 | 1 | 0 | 1 | 0 | 0.681 | 0.152 | JPN, KOR |
| 0 | 0 | 1 | 1 | 0 | 1 | 0.869 | 0.615 | FRA, IRE |
| 0 | 0 | 1 | 1 | 1 | 1 | 0.831 | 0.521 | CAN, ESP, GRB |
| 0 | 1 | 0 | 0 | 1 | 0 | 0.794 | 0.111 | NZL |
| 0 | 1 | 1 | 0 | 1 | 0 | 0.786 | 0.203 | AUS, USA |
| 1 | 0 | 0 | 1 | 0 | 1 | 0.984 | 0.944 | FIN |
| 1 | 0 | 1 | 0 | 1 | 0 | 0.758 | 0.014 | ISR |
| 1 | 1 | 0 | 0 | 1 | 0 | 0.790 | 0.018 | ITA |
| 1 | 1 | 0 | 1 | 0 | 1 | 0.999 | 0.996 | AUT, GER |
| 1 | 1 | 1 | 0 | 0 | 0 | 0.891 | 0.243 | ICE |
| 1 | 1 | 1 | 1 | 0 | 1 | 0.945 | 0.886 | BEL, DEN, NLD, NOR, SWE, CHE |

*Table 8.2*      *Sufficient solution – environment*

| Solution | Consistency | PRI | Coverage | Unique coverage | Cases |
|---|---|---|---|---|---|
| ~MHINT*EDUCTERT*KOFGLOB | 0.838 | 0.666 | 0.435 | 0.164 | FRA, IRE, CAN, ESP, GBR |
| MHINT*~EDUCTERT*KOFGLOB*~GINI | 0.989 | 0.972 | 0.347 | 0.036 | FIN, AUT, GER |
| MHINT*MHPART*KOFGLOB*~GINI | 0.954 | 0.909 | 0.522 | 0.006 | AUT, GER, BEL, DEN, NLD, NOR, SWE, CHE |

*Note*: The intermediate sufficient solution had a consistency 0.873, and a coverage of 0.760

The second pathway is a combination of highly integrative government, lower tertiary education, higher globalization and lower income inequality. It covers three countries only, but with very high consistency.

The third pathway combines highly integrative government with higher participative government, higher globalization and lower income inequality. It covers eight countries, so has the highest raw coverage score (but a low unique coverage score because of overlaps with the other solution pathways). This solution pathway has a very high consistency score but one case deviant for consistency – Belgium.

The conservative solution is identical to the intermediate one above, but the parsimonious solution is somewhat simpler, being based on two pathways only – EDUCTERT*KOFGLOB (which effectively combines the first and second pathways above) and MHINT*KOFGLOB*~GINI, which simplifies the third pathway a little.

As well as the three cases deviant for consistency (Canada, Ireland and Belgium), there are two cases deviant for coverage – Japan and Australia.

We can see the relative positioning of the countries in relation to one another in terms of the sufficient solution term and the set membership of high EPI scoring countries as follows:

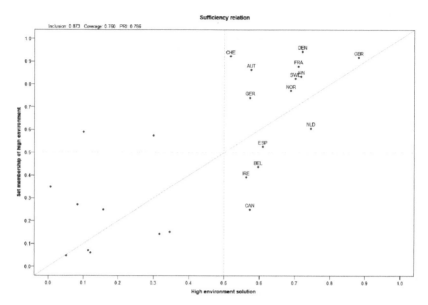

*Figure 8.3      Sufficient solution – environment*

The chart shows the three cases deviant for consistency in the bottom right quadrant.

## COMPARISON OF CLUSTER ANALYSIS AND QCA SOLUTIONS

If we compare the intermediate sufficient solution with the cluster analyses, then, with the exception of one small cluster of countries, there appears to be a strong relationship.

In terms of Ward.D linkage, all the countries on the left-hand side of the clustering appear in the QCA sufficient solution, including Belgium, which is deviant for consistency. On the right-hand side, there are three countries in the high-solution term (the UK, France and Spain), all of which are clustered closely together, but with none of the rest of the countries on the right-hand 'fork' of the dendrogram in the solution. The two other countries that are deviant for consistency (Canada and Ireland) also appear on the right-hand side of the dendrogram, but so do the two countries deviant for coverage (Australia and Japan). As such, the Ward.D clustering seems to map clearly onto the intermediate sufficient solution.

In terms of complete linkage, all the countries on the left-hand side of the clustering appear in the sufficient solution with the exception of Iceland, but with Belgium, which also appeared on the left-hand side of the Ward linkage dendrogram, but which is deviant for consistency, also appearing. On the right-hand side, the clustering of the UK, France and Spain, all of which appear in the sufficient solution, again appears. Once again Canada and Ireland, both of which are also deviant for consistency, and Australia and Japan, which are deviant for coverage, also appear on the right-hand side.

Overall, then, both clustering linkage methods appear to be consistent with one another, as well as with the QCA solutions.

## DISCUSSION

Of the three sufficient solution pathways, the third has the highest coverage as well as being arguably the most theoretically powerful, being made up of highly integrative and participative government, lower income inequality and higher globalization. These countries appear to have a coherent governance structure for confronting climate change. Countries with the combination of these factors appear to have a coherent governance structure for confronting climate change

Two of the countries in the third solution pathway, Austria and Germany, also appear in the second, presenting there a slightly different mix of causal factors based on highly integrative government and lower income inequality (which we might have expected), but also lower levels of tertiary education and higher globalization. Higher levels of tertiary education appear in only one of the solution pathways, and then the least consistent of the three. It appears to be less relevant as a causal factor than either higher globalization or lower income inequality.

The first solution pathway is the most unique, but also the least consistent, being made up of lower levels of integrative government, higher tertiary education and higher levels of globalization. However, two of the cases in this solution (Ireland and Canada) are deviant for consistency. From the perspective of someone living in the UK, however, it is good to see my own country finally appearing in one of the New Giant sufficient solutions, but the UK clearly has some distance to go in terms of addressing the challenges of the future.

The sufficient solution had three cases deviant for consistency: Ireland, Canada and Belgium. Ireland appears on the same truth table row as France, and in the first solution pathway with lower integrative government, higher tertiary education and higher globalization. Ireland is ranked sixteenth out of 120 countries in the environmental performance index, so in the top 20 worldwide. However, amongst the nations here, it is fifteenth out of the 24 countries, and so falls in the set of low performance. This may seem unfair, but it is important to assess Ireland in the context of countries that are similar to it; and amongst those, Ireland is doing relatively poorly. It scores well for the vitality of its ecosystem, but relatively poorly for environmental health with a weakness around waste management.

Canada is on the same truth table row as Spain and the United Kingdom, both of which out-perform it in terms of the EPI. Canada is placed thirty-eighth in the world in the environmental performance index, and so is more clearly falling behind similar countries in terms of its overall performance. Similar to Ireland, Canada has a strong and vibrant ecosystem, but it is singled out (alongside some other countries) in terms of its greenhouse gas emissions in the EPI report, which says, 'Countries in the Global West in general – but particularly Australia, Canada, and the United States – exhibit some of the worst performance in GHG emissions per capita due to high levels of consumption' (p.2). This quote makes a clear link to earlier discussions around the link between environmental degradation and consumerism. Canada is also ranked ninetieth in the world in terms of its biodiversity and habitat, where it is singled out again as a 'laggard' (p.89), is a hundred-and-tenth in terms of its ecosystem services, and eighty-ninth in terms of its fisheries score. Across these areas, then, it has fallen behind many of the other nations in this dataset.

Belgium is placed on a truth table row along with a range of very high performing countries – Denmark, the Netherlands, Norway, Sweden and Switzerland – but is the worst performing of them all. Belgium in the top 20 of countries in the world in terms of the overall EPI measure, but compared with many of the other countries here, and especially those on the same truth table row, has ground to make up. It is ranked globally seventeenth for environmental health, and twentieth in terms of ecosystem vitality. Perhaps more concerningly, its greenhouse gas performance appears to be worsening over time. Belgium only just falls into the top 100 in the world for ecosystem services and its scores for air quality, heavy metals, and sanitation and drinking water put it at the bottom of the top 20 countries in the world, even though it scores well for waste management and pollution emissions.

As such, Ireland, Canada and Belgium appear to have specific challenges that they need to face in order to improve to the highest standards of environmental protection.

There are also two countries that achieve a very high environmental performance index despite not falling into the QCA sufficient solution, and so are deviant for coverage.

Japan has the same mix of causal factors as Korea, but out-performs the latter by some distance across the categories in the environmental performance index. Japan is the highest-rated country in its own region across most of the measures in the EPI, and is singled out as one of the leading 'non-western' countries in the world. Japan, then, is exceptional in its region and in terms of its causal factors in this report, and there are strong hints in the EPI report of

Japan being an early mover in terms of recognizing the challenges that consumerism were bringing.

Australia has been an outlier case for most of this book. It is important, however, to note (as the report does) that the EPI 2020 does not incorporate the extraordinary bushfires in Australia at the end of 2019, which resulted in massive environmental damage. Despite its high overall performance, Australia does poorly in ecosystem services and its greenhouse gas emissions. Australia falls just on the margin between high and low performing countries in the EPI, and it seems likely that, once the result of the bushfires is accounted for, it may well fall into the low set. Australia, then, despite the huge advantages it has, may be in danger of falling behind the best-performing countries. If Australia has succeeded in many of the chapters of this book despite its combination of causal factors, its environmental performance seems to be the outcome that is most under threat.

## CONCLUSION

This chapter has explored the patterns of causal factors that the countries most successful in protecting the environmental have in common. If there is a New Giant that is most urgent of all, it is this one. The world has been rightly focused on the COVID-19 pandemic in 2020 and 2021, but unless we do more to confront the massive challenge that environmental degradation presents, the consequences could be catastrophic.

A clear link is made in the Environment Protection Index report between economic development and measures, such as those for greenhouse gases. As economies grow, there is greater potential for environmental harm. However, some countries are finding ways of alleviating that damage, and it is crucial that we learn from them.

In the QCA sufficient solutions, higher levels of globalization were present in all three solution terms, again emphasizing that globalization, in itself, is not automatically a social ill. What matters is the way that globalization is managed. The sufficient solution term with the highest coverage, and which has very high consistency, combines higher globalization with highly integrative government, higher participative government and lower levels of income inequality. Where governments combine these governance factors, countries seem to perform well in terms of environmental protection. This would suggest that inclusive and participative democracy, more equal levels of redistribution and a global outlook combine in a way from which other countries should be looking to learn.

If higher levels of globalization are present in all three sufficient solutions, lower income inequality is present in two of them, as is highly integrative government (although the first solution pathway includes lower integrative government as a factor). Within QCA it is the combination of factors that is important, but the presence of these factors underlines their importance in terms of environmental protection.

Looking beyond the QCA solutions, and incorporating them into the discussion that began this chapter, if countries should be considering both the way they are governed and how they redistribute, we also need stronger international agreements around climate change and environmental protection. Groups such as the G7, which at the time of writing has outlined an agreement around international taxation, have a role in leading on this as those countries, because of the links between international development and environmental impact, are amongst those doing the most harm. There is clearly a need for enforceable international targets with sanctions for countries breaching them, and support for countries that are still developing. If we can put together inter-national agreements around taxation, we can also do this for the environment in stronger forms than we have so far achieved. Countries that are lagging behind need to have stronger pressure applied, and an international community that is more prepared to act if they continue to pollute.

A further factor is the very mixed messaging that is present around climate change. There is a difficult mix of established interests seeking to undermine agreement, which might damage industries that are significant polluters, and of the sheer complexity of the science of environmental protection. Although the Environmental Performance Index does a good job of presenting its data, looking at how the composite measures are compiled quickly takes us into a world of acronyms and measures about which there is very little under-standing beyond those who specialize in this area. Although most of us are engaged in recycling and want to know what more we can do, education and public knowledge about the environment remains relatively poor. When com-bined with lobby groups that are trying to protect industries struggling with increased regulation, this can create a toxic context of disinformation in which environmental debates take place, as well as space for populist politicians to exploit people who are scared of losing their jobs (Hochschild 2016). We need to do better, in terms of education, and in supporting industries to transition to greener forms.

Finally, there are still two countries that have performed strongly against all our Five Giants: Norway and Sweden. The next chapter, the conclusion, will explore what we can learn from them, and their mix of causal factors.

## NOTE

1.   Available at https://epi.yale.edu/ (accessed on 12 November 2021).

# 9. Conclusion to *Welfare States in the 21st Century*

## INTRODUCTION

This book had two main aims. The first was to identify the New Giants confronting the world, updating Beveridge's original 'Giants', which he identified in 1942, to the very different context of the 2020s, 80 years on from his original report. In so doing, the New Giants had to both link to Beveridge's original selections, in order to have continuity with them (otherwise they wouldn't really be New Giants), as well as to be global in scope, and so being beyond what individuals and perhaps even most governments have the power to influence.

After a lengthy discussion in Chapters 1 and 2, Five New Giants – those of Inequality (replacing Want), Preventable Mortality (replacing Disease), Democratic Crisis (replacing Ignorance), Job Quality (replacing Idleness) and Environmental Degradation (replacing Squalor) were chosen. All of these are key challenges facing the world, but also have some countries clearly doing better than others in confronting them, and so presenting the opportunity for us to learn lessons from them.

In terms of working out what the most successful countries appear to have in common, Qualitative Comparative Analysis (QCA) was selected as the book's method as it allows a rigorous analysis of a relatively small dataset (in order for countries to be as comparable as possible), also allowing for different countries to have different pathways to high achievement, and for complex patterns of causality to exist. Given the crucial role that developed countries play across the New Giants, but also because of pragmatic issues such as reliable data availability, 24 developed countries were included in the book's sample.

QCA requires data to be calibrated into sets, and in order to compare its results with those from the 'raw' measures, the book also conducted cluster analysis using two linkage methods, Ward and complete linkage, which provided an additional means of representing the data (using dendrograms) as well as a further comparison with the QCA's sufficient solutions.

The book's causal factors and outcome measures were made up of a mix of social and political factors deemed most relevant to the particular New

Giant under consideration. All chapters included a measure of the extent of integrative government, and one for tertiary education participation in order to facilitate cross-chapter comparison.

The next section summarizes and compares the results for countries that performed best in relation to each of the Five Giants.

## FACTORS IN SOLUTIONS AND WHAT WE CAN LEARN FROM THEM

QCA presents results that are equifinal, generating different pathways or causal recipes to the outcomes with which we are concerned. However, including all the solution pathways present in the book risks presenting an overwhelming amount of data. As such, Table 9.1 considers, for each of the Five Giants, the causal factors for the pathway with the highest coverage or unique coverage of countries, and in most cases an additional pathway where a high degree of equifinality that covers several countries appears to exist. This gives us a means of summarizing the solutions and comparing across them to see what the most successful countries have in common and difference.

The table appears to suggest a significant agreement about the causal factors that lead to strong performance against the New Giants. Including integrative government (MHINT) in all chapters of the book seems justified as it appears in a range of solution terms, and in one case only (the only one in the grid) appears in its low form (in the Environment 2 solution, where it is marked with '~' in common with the rest of the book). Higher levels of tertiary education appear in six of the nine solution terms, also emphasizing the importance of this factor, and justifying its role in the book.

Other factors are not included in all the different chapters, but, where they do appear, seem consistently important. This is especially true for lower levels of income inequality (~GINI) which is consistently important for strong democracy and job quality, and is in what is the most substantively important environment protection solution in Chapter 8.

As such, there appears to be evidence that countries performing well across the Five Giants often have integrative government and higher levels of tertiary education in common. As well as this, a recurrent theme has been that higher levels of globalization do not have to lead to poor outcomes – countries that perform well often have higher levels of globalization, but are mitigating against its worst effects, and harnessing what is good. From the perspective of the United Kingdom, where globalization has often been portrayed as such a threat, this is a liberating message. The effects of higher levels of globalization depend on what governments do in response to them; they do not inevitably lead to greater inequalities or poorer job quality.

*Table 9.1*   Factors in common across main sufficient solutions

| | Inequality 1 | Inequality 2 | Prevent mort | Democracy 1 | Democracy 2 | Job Quality 1 | Job Quality 2 | Environment 1 | Environment 2 |
|---|---|---|---|---|---|---|---|---|---|
| MHINT | X | | X | X | | X | | X | ? |
| EDUCTERT | | X | X | X | X | | X | | X |
| KOFGLOB | X | X | | | X | | X | X | X |
| PUBSOC | X | X | | | | | X | | |
| ~LJIPFU | | | X | | | | | | |
| ~GINI | | | | X | X | X | X | X | |
| GDPCAP | | | | X | X | | | | |
| MHPART | | | | | | | | X | |

## CONSISTENTLY HIGH-PERFORMING COUNTRIES AND WHAT WE CAN LEARN FROM THEM

We can also explore the same QCA solutions to consider which countries have performed most consistently well in terms of the New Giants. The results are presented in Table 9.2.

Countries that are deviant for consistency in QCA solutions are not included in the table above (as they do not achieve a high score in the relevant New Giant), neither are those that are deviant for coverage (as they do not fit with the QCA solutions presented above).

As the book has already noted, Norway and Sweden are the two countries that both appear in QCA solutions and achieve high scores for all of the New Giants. Denmark and Switzerland (CHE) are slightly behind, falling just short in terms of preventable mortality in each case. For preventable mortality, Denmark was deviant for consistency but in the same solution pathway as Norway and Sweden, while Switzerland was deviant for coverage. As such, Switzerland actually also meets the challenge of all the New Giants, even though it does not have causal factors for preventable mortality that are sufficiently consistent to appear in the QCA solutions.

There are a range of countries that do not appear in the table above at all. In some cases, this is because they do successfully meet one or more of the New Giants, but do not have consistent causal factors in relation to them (with Australia being the obvious case here), but in others it is simply because they do not reach a strong score for any of the New Giants (with the USA falling into that category). It is certainly disheartening, though, to see the United Kingdom only performing well in relation to one New Giant. In a time when the UK voted to leave the European Union to be better able to pursue its own goals, it seems it has a great deal to learn from northern European nations especially.

It is remarkable that so many of the countries that perform well across all of the Five Giants are so (relatively) geographically close to one another. Norway and Sweden share the same peninsula, and just across the sea at the southern tip of Sweden we find Denmark. This small cluster of nations comprises three of the four highest performing in terms of the New Giants, suggesting there is a shared historical and cultural background to the success of these countries in being able to confront the challenges the world currently faces. This success appears to be based around a shared approach to highly integrative government system, a highly skilled workforce, with open economies that are successful in the global marketplace, and they have a tradition of being actively redistributive so that the inequalities of income present in other countries do not appear. Norway, Sweden and Denmark have higher levels of public social

Table 9.2    *Countries achieving strongly in each of the New Giants*

| | Inequality 1 | Inequality 2 | Prevent mort | Democracy 1 | Democracy 2 | Job quality 1 | Job quality 2 | Environment 1 | Environment 2 |
|---|---|---|---|---|---|---|---|---|---|
| AUT | X | | | | | X | | X | |
| BEL | X | X | | | | X | X | | |
| DEN | X | X | | X | X | X | X | X | |
| ESP | | | | | | | | | X |
| FIN | X | | | | | X | | | |
| FRA | | X | | | | X | X | | X |
| GER | X | | | | | X | | X | |
| GBR | | | | | | | | | X |
| ICE | | | X | X | | X | | | |
| IRE | | X | | | X | | | | |
| ISR | | | X | | | | | | |
| NLD | | | | X | X | X | | X | |
| NOR | X | X | X | X | X | X | X | X | |
| SWE | X | X | X | X | X | X | X | X | |
| CHE | X | X | | X | X | X | X | X | |

expenditure, emphasizing their commitment to redistribute, while also providing strong public services. These factors combine to create a context in which the global challenges identified in this book are being confronted, and it is hard not to regard them as presenting a template from which the rest of the world can learn.

In addition to Norway, Denmark and Sweden, Switzerland, which is a little further away geographically, and which has a somewhat different history and culture, also has a very strong performance across the New Giants. Switzerland does not offer as consistent a template as the other three countries, but does share a great deal with them. Switzerland also has a highly integrative government, a high-skill workforce, operates successfully in the global economy, and has higher public social expenditure. Switzerland also has relatively low-income inequality, but unlike Denmark, Norway and Sweden, is highly federal. This appears to demonstrate that it is possible for governments with both centralized and decentralized forms to be effective in confronting the New Giants provided they have the other factors in common. Switzerland then offers a slightly different template, but one that has a great deal in common with its three successful European neighbours.

## OTHER SUCCESSFUL COUNTRIES WITH LESS CONSISTENT SOLUTIONS

Denmark, Norway, Switzerland and Sweden offer the outline of a template that appears to consistently be successful in confronting the New Giants. However, QCA is a method that presents results including cases deviant for coverage – countries that are successful in terms of the New Giants, but don't appear in solutions because other countries sharing their causal factors do not achieve the same degree of success. The cases deviant for coverage for each New Giant are shown in Table 9.3.

*Table 9.3      High-performing countries outside of solutions and New Giant performance*

|      | Inequality | Preventable mortality | Democracy | Job quality | Environmental degradation |
|------|-----------|-----------------------|-----------|-------------|---------------------------|
| AUS  |           | X                     |           | X           | X                         |
| CAN  | X         |                       | X         | X           |                           |
| CHE  |           | X                     |           |             |                           |
| NZL  |           |                       | X         |             |                           |
| JPN  |           |                       |           |             | X                         |

Australia and Canada, then, are the two countries most often deviant for coverage. In addition to this, Australia appears in the solution term of high democracy (so is not deviant for coverage), such that it is achieving high scores for four of the five New Giants (only falling short on inequality) – the same level of overall achievement as Denmark. Canada does not achieve high performance in relation to the New Giants of Preventable Mortality or Climate Change, but does reach this level for the other three.

Australia, as previous chapters have outlined, is an unusual country, and one that is difficult to characterize in typologies of welfare systems (Esping-Andersen 1990). Its history shows a shared heritage with the United Kingdom especially, but its geographic location means that it is increasingly strongly linked with other parts of the world. It has an economy that is dynamic, but where traditional industries still play a significant role. However, it also has higher levels of inequality than the other countries achieving strong performance across the five New Giants. Australia does have a very different pattern of causal factors from Denmark, Norway, Sweden and Switzerland, but the key thing is that Australia is an exception; other countries with similar patterns of inequality, federal government that is not highly integrative, and with lower levels of public social expenditure are nowhere near as successful. Australia, therefore, does not offer a template in the same way as other countries in the book, sharing most of its causal factor with nations performing poorly against the New Giants.

Canada, as outlined above, is high achieving in relation to three of the five New Giants, but, in common with Australia, has patterns of causal factors that are shared by other nations not as successful. Canada does not have highly integrative government or higher public social expenditure, and also has relatively high-income inequality, three factors that it has in common with Australia. Both countries, however, also have a great deal in common in terms of causal factors with the USA, which is one of the worst-performing nations in terms of the New Giants, and which means that the factors that they share do not consistently form the basis of a sufficient QCA solution. Canada, as with Australia, therefore appears to be an exception in terms of its causal factors, and not a template for other countries to follow.

## CONCLUSION

The book's final message, then, is that the New Giants represent global challenges to all nations. The developed nations of the world, with which this book has been largely concerned, have a special responsibility in confronting the New Giants because of the resources they command, but also because of their own roles in contributing to the challenges that the New Giants represent. It is easy to feel, because of the scale of these challenges, that there is nothing any of us can do. However, this is very much not the case.

The countries that are most successful in confronting the New Giants consistently have patterns of social and political causal factors both supported by empirical data and explainable in theoretical terms. It is important to treat the factors in that causal combination as being linked to one another to create a reinforcing circle, rather than something from which other nations can pick and choose. That combination of factors is based on integrative government, which incorporates a wide range of interests rather than excluding them; has a highly educated public; is committed to redistribution through higher social expenditure, leading to lower levels of income inequality; and is highly successful in competing in the global economy. Norway, Sweden and Switzerland offer us a template towards confronting the New Giants, most of which is shared by Denmark, but which falls just short of their level of achievement across all of them. For some countries, this mix of factors is a considerable distance from the one they currently have in place. If those other countries' performance is falling far short in relation to the New Giants, and unless they are prepared to consider change, the evidence from this book would suggest they are at risk of not confronting the New Giants.

There are some nations that seem to succeed despite their current patterns of causal factors (especially Australia, but also Canada), and the reasons for those countries' successes is clearly a source of potential future research. However, given that Australia and Canada have so much in common with nations that perform significantly worse than them, they offer less a template for success than a measure of the highest possible success that those factors can provide. If we are to confront the New Giants, we need to aim for causal factors that more consistently lead to strong outcome solutions in relation to them, and the patterns of factors that even more successful nations consistently demonstrate suggests what are likely to be successful patterns of social and political factors we would do well to follow more closely.

# 10. Epilogue: the New Giants and COVID-19

## INTRODUCTION

This book was written in 2020 and 2021, and so during the COVID-19 pandemic. The proposal, however, had been submitted and approved before then. None of us could have imagined how significant a role the pandemic would play in all our lives, or the extent of death and illness that would result from it. My strong hope is that the virus will mutate into the background of winter illness, or that a global vaccination programme will halt its spread.

In a book about major societal challenges, this led to dilemmas about whether to include the pandemic or not. At the time of writing this chapter (June 2021), although huge progress has been made in terms of the development of vaccinations, not all countries have access to them, and new variants of the virus are still appearing. Things are fragile. The story of COVID-19 still has some way to go.

My first thought was not to include the pandemic in this book as I wanted to focus on long-term challenges, and although the virus has absorbed us completely for the last eighteen months, changing the lives of everyone, leading to deaths on an unimaginable scale and leaving many of those who have recovered from it with longer-term health problems, COVID-19 does not represent the same kind of challenge as the other New Giants explored in this book.

However, the virus does pose at least one additional question. Are the countries most successfully confronting the other New Giants also the best performing in relation to the pandemic? If it is the case, as some commentators are suggesting, that pandemics will now become more widespread because of increased international travel and additional pressure on the global ecosystem, perhaps COVID-19 can give us clues as to which countries might be most able to deal with such challenges in the future.

This chapter takes several of the causal factors from previous chapters that were at the core of the solutions for the most successful countries, and considers whether they also seem to have led to success in dealing with the pandemic. Answering this question is challenging in terms of data, as I will make clear, but we are able to draw some preliminary conclusions and relate them to the causal patterns of the previous chapters.

## CAUSAL FACTORS

In other work I have utilized this book's method to consider the relationship between a range of factors linked to increased risk from COVID-19 (including obesity rates and the proportion of the population of elderly people, along with international travel levels at the beginning of the pandemic and income inequality) (Greener 2021a). In that research, both inequality and COVID tests per case, rather than levels of testing per se, were the most important factors consistently present in the countries that were most successful in dealing with COVID-19 during its first six months. This chapter considers COVID-19 with a different lens to that work, but also taking some of the findings from that previous research into account. Previous chapters in this book have confirmed the strong case for including income inequality in comparative analysis, and the degree of integrative government, and the level of public social expenditure were also consistently important factors that the countries most successful in confronting the New Giants have in common.

This chapter brings these elements together, considering income inequality, the level of integrative government, and public social expenditure, but also COVID tests per case as its causal factors. It sought to include all of the countries included in other chapters in the book, but it had to exclude Sweden, for which reliable testing data are not available (and the Swedish case has to be considered separately as that country has taken a very unusual approach to dealing with the pandemic, which has not been successful).

The outcome measure for COVID-19 is difficult to choose. The ideal would probably be a cross-national dataset accurately capturing excess mortality during the pandemic, but this comes with problems because, as the pandemic goes beyond one year, low excess mortality in the second year of the pandemic could still be due to the high number of COVID-19 deaths in year one. This is because, in countries that experienced very high death rates in the first year of the pandemic (such as the UK), many of those with vulnerable health may have had their deaths brought forward in time by the virus. Excess mortality rates will, I suspect, eventually become the gold standard for measuring COVID-19 deaths, but we are still a long way from having reliable data in respect of them.

Given the complex data situation, the best measures we probably presently have are the COVID-19 death number measures being presented by nations (albeit with some differences in counting and method), which are being collated on websites such as the Oxford University COVID response tracker[1] and ourworldindata.com. The data are imperfect, but they do give us an indicator of which countries have done relatively well or badly in outline, allowing us to calibrate the data for QCA, while accepting that some cases at the margins of the calibration points might not be as accurately measured as we would like.

The next challenge is to choose a point or points in time at which to measure COVID deaths. For this chapter I chose 30 June 2020, as this seems to represent a time around six months after China first reported cases of the virus, and at this point most countries in the dataset had experienced a 'first wave' of infections. This date therefore allows us to consider how well the countries in the dataset managed to respond to the initial challenge of the virus, and perhaps, then, to further pandemics. Beyond June 2020, the virus has had further waves, but at different times in different countries, and it becomes extremely difficult to find data points that are as well synchronized in terms of their COVID death (and case) data. Even at 30/6, countries such as Israel and the United States are out of synchronization with most other countries, and this needs to be borne in mind.

It is also possible to measure COVID-19 cases as well as deaths. I have not done this here as the correlation between deaths and cases at 30/6 r is 0.79 (p 0.0000063) for raw data or r is 0.73 (p. 0.000071 for calibrated data). As such, including both factors is useful in terms of the cluster analysis as it can be used to add an additional weight to the outcome data, but performing QCA using both outcomes adds relatively little to the chapter's findings.

## CLUSTER ANALYSIS

As with other chapters in the book, the data can be first explored using cluster analysis. The Ward method of clustering produces the diagram presented in Figure 10.1. On the left-hand side of the diagram is a familiar group of countries (Denmark, Norway, Germany, Austria and Finland). These are joined by Belgium, Iceland, the Netherlands and Switzerland, which is a cluster also similar to previous chapters, but with the addition of Israel, which is less typically linked to them.

On the right-hand side the countries are far more mixed geographically, with the USA and New Zealand appearing separate from the rest of the countries, but with less obviously in common between many of the countries closely linked together.

Complete clustering produces the solution presented in Figure 10.2.

In complete clustering, the countries are more mixed at a higher level, but fairly consistent with Ward clustering at lower levels. Denmark, Norway, Germany, Austria and Finland are closely clustered (as with Ward), but here are joined first by Belgium, then with Italy, France and Ireland as well as Iceland, the Netherlands and Switzerland, with Israel moving further away but Italy, France and Ireland closer than under Ward clustering. The USA and New Zealand retain a position as most distance from the rest of the countries.

Although the diagram shape appears rather different to the Ward clustering at first glance, looking again, the clusters of countries, at least at lower levels, are very similar.

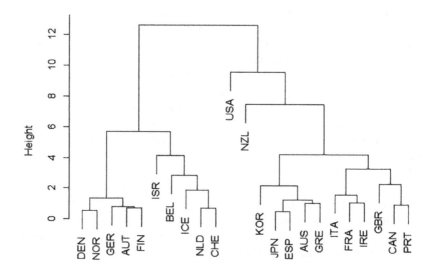

*Figure 10.1      Ward clustering – COVID-19*

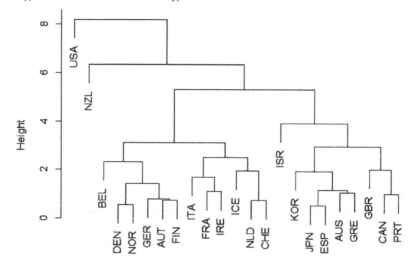

*Figure 10.2      Complete clustering – COVID-19*

# QCA

Moving on to QCA, the first stage is to look for necessary conditions in the data. No necessary conditions were found with both high consistency and high relevance, but ~GINI+~PUBSOC (lower GINI or lower public social expenditure) was the highest scorer in those terms with a consistency of 0.921 and a relevance of 0.503, but with that relevance score probably too low to be included. From the discussion above, we might have expected lower income inequality to be linked to lower COVID mortality, but lower levels of public social expenditure appear less obvious. This combination was therefore not included as a necessary condition in the subsequent calculations.

The truth table is presented in Table 10.1.

The truth table here presented some dilemmas. The first and last rows have consistency scores above 0.8, but relatively low PRI scores so were excluded from the sufficient solution for that reason. The fourth row (AUT, BEL, GER and CHE) has a consistency that is a little below 0.8, but the PRI score was higher than the first or last row, and so the decision was made to include this row.

Directional expectations were set for higher tests per case and lower income inequality, in line with my own previous research.

The intermediate sufficient solution is presented in Table 10.2.

The first solution pathway combines lower income inequality with higher levels of integrative government, and covers nine countries. However, two of them (Austria and Belgium) are deviant for consistency.

The second solution pathway combines lower income inequality with higher tests per case, and covers five countries, but one (Ireland) is deviant for consistency.

The third solution pathway combines lower integrative government with higher tests per case, and lower public social expenditure, and covers three countries.

In addition to the cases that are deviant for consistency, three are deviant for coverage so do not appear in the solution above, despite these countries achieving relatively low COVID mortality. These countries are Greece, Japan and Spain.

The conservative solution is identical to the intermediate solution, suggesting that the directional expectations included had little effect in the calculation of the intermediate solution. The parsimonious solution has two pathways only – the first is the same as the first in the intermediate solution above, but the second comprises ~MHINT*TESTCASE only, effectively combining the second two pathways in the intermediate solution as a result.

*Table 10.1*　　　*Truth table – COVID-19*

| GINI | MHINT | TESTCASE | PUBSOC | OUT | Consist | PRI | Cases |
|------|-------|----------|--------|-----|---------|-----|-------|
| 0 | 0 | 0 | 1 | 0 | 0.800 | 0.468 | FRA |
| 0 | 0 | 1 | 1 | 1 | 0.808 | 0.556 | IRE |
| 0 | 1 | 0 | 0 | 1 | 0.880 | 0.672 | NLD |
| 0 | 1 | 0 | 1 | 1 | 0.785 | 0.543 | AUT, BEL, GER, CHE |
| 0 | 1 | 1 | 0 | 1 | 0.890 | 0.675 | ICE |
| 0 | 1 | 1 | 1 | 1 | 0.886 | 0.771 | DEN, GER, NOR |
| 1 | 0 | 0 | 0 | 0 | 0.611 | 0.447 | CAN, GRE, JPN, PRT, ESP, GBR |
| 1 | 0 | 0 | 1 | 0 | 0.630 | 0.226 | USA |
| 1 | 0 | 1 | 0 | 1 | 0.836 | 0.742 | AUS, KOR, NZL |
| 1 | 1 | 0 | 0 | 0 | 0.736 | 0.252 | ISR |
| 1 | 1 | 0 | 1 | 0 | 0.845 | 0.433 | ITA |

*Table 10.2*       *Intermediate sufficient solution*

| Solution | Consistency | PRI | Coverage | Unique coverage | Cases |
|----------|-------------|-----|----------|-----------------|-------|
| ~GINI*MHI NT | 0.801 | 0.676 | 0.478 | 0.117 | AUT, BEL, DEN, FIN, GER, ICE, NLD, NOR, CHE |
| ~GINI*TES TCASE | 0.843 | 0.738 | 0.401 | 0.015 | DEN, FIN, ICE, IRE, NOR |
| ~MHINT*T ESTCASE* ~PUBSOC | 0.848 | 0.768 | 0.345 | 0.161 | AUS, KOR, NZL |

*Note*: This solution has a consistency of 0.791, and a coverage of 0.680

## COMPARING THE CLUSTER ANALYSIS AND QCA RESULTS

There is a close correspondence between the first pathway of the QCA sufficient solution and the left hand of the Ward clustering diagram. The first pathway contains Austria, Belgium, Denmark, Finland, Germany, Iceland, the Netherlands, Norway and Switzerland, all of which are located to the left of the dendrogram. There is one additional country on the left-hand side of the dendrogram, Israel, which was not in the set of lower COVID mortality countries, and the two cases that are deviant for consistency in the QCA solution (Austria and Belgium) are not differentiated from those that achieve lower COVID mortality.

The second intermediate solution pathway has some crossover with the first, with Denmark, Finland, Iceland and Norway also appearing there. The second pathway, however, adds Ireland, but with Ireland deviant for consistency, and so it seems there is little to be gained from this addition, and so no additional insight from comparing the clustering solutions to this pathway's QCA solution.

The third intermediate solution pathway includes Australia, Korea and New Zealand. These countries are not especially close in the Ward clustering, and although they are all on the right-hand side, the clustering would suggest that,while they appear in a QCA solution, there are significant differences between them when all the causal factors are taken into account.

As noted earlier, the complete clustering method produces similar clustering at the micro level, with Austria, Belgium, Denmark, Finland, Germany and Norway all very close to one another, and close to Iceland, the Netherlands and Switzerland. However, the left-hand side of the dendrogram also includes Italy, France and Ireland as being close to these other countries. Italy and France have a complex combination of causal factors: they were ruled out of the QCA sufficient solution because of simultaneous set relations (indicated by a relatively low PRI score in the truth table), whereas Ireland were included in the second QCA sufficient solution but as a case deviant for coverage. However, while Ward clustering includes Israel on the left-hand side of the dendrogram, complete clustering moves it away from the other countries in QCA solution, so seems to reflect this aspect of the data more helpfully.

The second sufficient solution pathway, as noted above, adds relatively little to the first, and we have already considered the role of Ireland in the complete clustering method. This leaves the third pathway solution, with New Zealand, Australia and Korea still not being located very closely to one another in either of the dendrograms.

In all, then, although the clustering diagrams correspond strongly to the first pathway of the QCA solution, especially using complete clustering linkage, and this pathway has the highest coverage in the intermediate solution. The third intermediate solution pathway, however, is not really supported by either method in the cluster analysis, suggesting that these countries have significant differences despite appearing in a single pathway in the QCA solution.

## DISCUSSION

Of the three intermediate sufficient solution pathways, the first and the third appear to be the most important, with the first having the highest coverage, and the third being very different from the first two.

The first sufficient solution pathway contains nine countries, but with two (Austria and Belgium) deviant for consistency. It consists of lower income inequality and highly integrative government, both of which are factors that consistently appear in the rest of the book. This suggests that these factors, which tend to combine in nations that do well across the New Giants (but which are closer to being necessary rather than sufficient across all five), are also present in countries that responded well to COVID in the first wave of the pandemic.

There are good theoretical reasons why this might have been the case. It certainly seems to be the case that the most deprived communities were especially affected by the pandemic (Boin, Lodge and Luesink 2020), and countries with lower levels of income inequality are likely to have faced less of a challenge in those terms. A highly integrative government could make rapid decision-making more difficult, but in the case of COVID-19, it does not seem to have harmed the pandemic response in most of the countries in the first solution pathway. The response of highly integrative governments might be contrasted with countries such as the United Kingdom, where it appears a relatively closed group of decision-makers did a poorer job in responding to the different dimensions of the crisis (Cairney 2021).

The success of Australia, Korea and New Zealand in the third sufficient solution pathway presents a very different list of causal factors: lower integrative government, lower public social expenditure but higher tests per COVID case. These three nations, however, responded to the pandemic in a very different way to the rest of those in the sample. They closed international travel borders, put in place strong quarantine processes, and had very high levels of testing per case. All three nations had a geographical advantage in being able to do this (not having open land borders), and made use of this advantage to prevent the transmission of the virus into their countries. It is worth reflecting, however, that other island nations did not respond in the same way, and did not enjoy the same kind of success in dealing with COVID-19. As such, it is perhaps best to regard Australia, Korea and New Zealand not in terms of their shared causal factors in this chapter, but in respect of the other factors outlined above that allowed their strong COVID response. The sufficient solution in this chapter, as with others in this book, is not perfect. It is unrealistic to expect a simple model to capture complex reality in its entirety, but we can abstract to a useful degree to look for the factors that countries which were more successful in first-wave COVID-19 have in common. There are three cases that are deviant for consistency, so appearing in the sufficient solution, but were not successful in their first-wave COVID-19 response, and three that were successful in first-wave COVID-19 response, but do not appear in the sufficient solution.

The three cases that are deviant for consistency are Austria, Belgium and Ireland. Austria and Belgium appear on the same truth table row as Germany and Switzerland. This means that these countries have both similar causal factors, and it is also the case that they are very close geographically to one another. Given the importance of containing the virus, and of the difficulty of doing this for these countries, it is perhaps more surprising that Switzerland and Germany were successful than that Austria and Belgium were not. This truth table row emphasizes the challenge that countries with large land-borders faced from the pandemic.

Ireland, in contrast, appears on its own truth table row, but is a case deviant for coverage in the second sufficient solution. Ireland has relatively low income inequality, and managed to put in place a robust testing regime, but still appears to have struggled with its COVID response. An early examination of the Irish response (Kennelly et al. 2020) suggests that most of the cases were clustered either in Dublin, or more generally along the border with Northern Ireland, where testing appears to have been much less widespread and rigorous. As such, Ireland may have struggled with a similar problem to the other countries deviant for consistency, that of containing the virus with a land border present.

Three countries were deviant for coverage – Greece, Japan and Spain. All three countries appear on a truth table row with a range of countries that have been less successful in their COVID response (including the UK), having higher income inequality, lower integrative government, lower testing per case, and lower public social expenditure. This combination of factors is theoretically, in many respects, the worst of all possible worlds. Despite this, however, these three countries succeeded where the others did not, and this is clearly a potential source of further research. We can say, however, that Japan's culture, where mask-wearing is more routine and a lack of physical contact with strangers (the custom of bowing rather than shaking hands) has been presented as a possible contributory factor in its initial case numbers being lower than in other countries. It is also the case unfortunately, that the comparative success of these three countries has not remained in place throughout the pandemic, suggesting that the three countries were in some way insulated from the initial transmission of the virus in a way that others were not.

It is also the case that one country that appears to have successfully addressed the New Giants through the book, and which we might have reasonably expected to be also successful in dealing with the challenge that COVID-19 offers, has struggled. Sweden decided to go down a rather unique path in its COVID-19 response, not engaging in a 'lockdown' strategy in the same way as other countries, and relying upon people to engage voluntarily with social distancing and other transmission prevention strategies. Sweden's response, which appeared to be based on allowing the virus to move through the population and so to achieve a kind of 'herd immunity', has been labelled a 'disaster' (Bjorklund and Ewing 2020). There were large numbers of deaths amongst vulnerable groups, especially those in care homes, and schools and nurseries remained open. Sweden appeared to lag behind other nations in its test and trace infrastructure, and did not put in place quarantine measures for travellers. As such, despite the significant advantages Sweden has in relation to its governmental structure and its lower level of inequality, it appears to have experienced a failure of governance and has not succeeded in building the COVID infrastructure that its more successful near-neighbours managed to put in place. The Swedish response to COVID-19 is worthy of significant investigation to better understand what went so wrong, but that is beyond the scope of what can be done in this book, especially at the time of writing.

## CONCLUSION

This book is not about COVID-19, and so this chapter appears after its main conclusion. It is also the case that, at present (mid-2021), the pandemic is far from over. Data are far from complete, and any findings have to be preliminary. To try to deal with some of these challenges, the chapter considered COVID-19 from a particular perspective – in relation to the initial response of governments to it. However, there are some overlaps, which appear in the first nine chapters. COVID-19 has fallen hardest on those who were already experiencing disadvantage, and so it is not surprising that lower inequality appears (along with highly integrative government) as central to the sufficient solution with the highest coverage and highest unique coverage. A combination of lower levels of inequality with a governmental structure based on including a range of stakeholders is credible both conceptually and empirically in dealing with a crisis, and that appears to have been borne out in relation to the pandemic.

It is equally credible that countries with lower levels of income inequality, which managed to put in place robust testing regimes, should also be successful. The second sufficient pathway solution highlights again that countries with lower gradients of income have been more successful where they also managed to respond quickly to the challenge of putting in place a regime of testing and tracing those affected by the virus. This makes theoretical sense, and is borne out by the evidence.

There was another route to responding to COVID-19 effectively in its first wave, that taken by Australia, South Korea and New Zealand, which involves robust testing, but also a factor more difficult to measure and beyond the scope of the comparative analysis here – preventing international travel. These three countries remain (at the time of writing) largely closed to international travel, taking advantage of their geographical locations to make sure that the virus is prevented from entering where at all possible, and contained (through a robust testing process, and if necessary, local lockdowns) where it does appear. Other countries that have similar geographical advantages, such as the UK, did not go down this route.

In all, many of the factors that have been highlighted in this book, when supplemented by a measure of COVID-19 responsiveness, the building of a testing regime that scaled with the degree of spread of the virus in the particular country, help explain the differential success of the countries considered here in the first wave COVID-19 fairly well. However, as noted above, there are some notable exceptions (including Sweden), and there was another route – based on border controls – that also led to success.

## NOTE

1.  https://www.bsg.ox.ac.uk/research/research-projects/covid-19-government -response-tracker (accessed on 12 November 2021).

# Bibliography

Abbott, Andrew. 1988. *The System of Professions: An Essay on the Division of Expert Labor*. Chicago, IL: University of Chicago Press.

Achen, Christopher, and Larry Bartels. 2016. *Democracy for Realists: Why Elections Do Not Produce Responsive Government*. London: Princeton University Press.

Atkinson, Tony. 1999. 'Beveridge and the 21st Century', pp.29–34 in *Ending Child Poverty: Popular Welfare for the 21st Century?*, edited by R. Walker. Bristol: Bristol University Press.

Babones, Salvatore. 2013. *Methods for Quantitative Macro-Comparative Research*. London: Sage.

Baldock, J. 2003. 'On Being a Welfare Consumer in a Consumer Society', *Social Policy and Society* 2(1):65–71.

Ball, S. 2017. *The Education Debate*. Bristol: Policy Press.

Bambra, C. 2007a. 'Defamilisation and Welfare State Regimes: A Cluster Analysis', *International Journal of Social Welfare* 16:326–38.

Bambra, C. 2007b. 'Going beyond The Three Worlds of Welfare Capitalism: Regime Theory and Public Health Research', *Journal of Epidemiology and Community Health* 61:1098–1102.

Bambra, C. 2017. *Health Divides: Where You Live Can Kill You*. Bristol: Policy Press.

Barber, B. 2004. *Strong Democracy: Participatory Politics for a New Age*. Oakland, CA: University of California Press.

Barber, B. 2007. *Consumed: How Markets Corrupt Children, Infantilize Adults and Swallow Citizens Whole*. London: W. W. Norton & Co.

Barber, M. 2007. *Instruction to Deliver: Tony Blair, the Public Services and the Challenge of Achieving Targets*. London: Portoco's Publishing.

Beck, U. 1992. *Risk Society: Towards A New Modernity*. London: Sage.

Beck, Ulrich, Anthony Giddens, and Scott Lash. 1994. *Reflexive Modernization: Politics, Tradition and Aesthetics in the Modern Social Order*. Cambridge: Polity.

Bevan, Gwyn, and Christopher Hood. 2006. 'What's Measured Is What Matters: Targets and Gaming in the English Public Health Care System', *Public Administration* 84(3):517–38.

Beveridge, W. 1942. *Social Insurance and Allied Services*. Vol. Cmnd 6404. London: HMSO.

Beveridge, William. 1909. *Unemployment: A Problem of Industry*. London: Longmans, Green & Co.

Bjorklund, Kelly, and Andrew Ewing. 2020. 'The Swedish COVID-19 Response Is a Disaster. It Shouldn't Be a Model for the Rest of the World', *Time*, October 14.

Boin, Arjen, Martin Lodge, and Marte Luesink. 2020. 'Learning from the COVID-19 Crisis: An Initial Analysis of National Responses', *Policy Design and Practice* 1–16. doi: 10.1080/25741292.2020.1823670.

Bormann, Nils-Christian. 2010. 'Patterns of Democracy and Its Critics', *Living Reviews in Democracy* (1):1–14.

Bregman, Rutger. 2017. *Utopia for Realists: And How We Can Get There*. London: Bloomsbury.

Butler, P. 2017. 'Large Rise in Takeaway Shops Highlights Dominance of Fast Food in Deprived Areas', *The Guardian*.

Cairney, Paul. 2021. 'The UK Government's COVID-19 Policy: What Does "Guided by the Science" Mean in Practice?' *Frontiers in Political Science* 3:624068. doi: 10.3389/fpos.2021.624068.

Case, Anne, and Angus Deaton. 2020. *Deaths of Despair and the Future of Capitalism*. Princeton, NJ: Princeton University Press.

Cerny, P. 1997. 'Paradoxes of the Competition State: The Dynamics of Political Globalization', *Government and Opposition* 32(2):251–74.

Chen, Wen-Hao, Tahsin Mehdi, Statistique Canada, and Direction des études analytiques. 2018. *Assessing Job Quality in Canada: A Multidimensional Approach*, available at http://publications.gc.ca/collections/collection_2018/statcan/11f0019m/11f0019m2018412-eng.pdf (accessed on 25 November 2021).

Chitty, C. 2004. *Education Policy in Britain*. Basingstoke: Palgrave Macmillan.

Coats, David. 2020. 'A New Beveridge', Fabian Society, available at https://fabians.org.uk/a-new-beveridge/ (accessed on 25 November 2021).

Commission on the Social Determinants of Health. 2008. *Commission on the Social Determinants of Health Final Report: Closing the Gap in a Generation: Health Equity through Action on the Social Determinants of Health*. Geneva: World Health Organization.

Cottam, Hilary. 2019. *Radical Help: How We Can Remake the Relationships between Us and Revolutionise the Welfare State*. London: Virago.

Crouch, C. 2004. *Post-Democracy*. Cambridge: Polity Press.

Daly, M., and K. Rake. 2003. *Gender and the Welfare State*. Cambridge: Polity Press.

Deaton, Angus. 2015. *The Great Escape: Health, Wealth and the Origins of Inequality*. Princeton, NJ: Princeton University Press.

Debeuf, Koert. 2020. 'Belgum Ends Two-Year Government Crisis with Fresh PM', *EU Observer*.

Dorling, Danny. 2015. *Injustice: Why Social Inequality Still Persists*. Bristol: Policy Press.

Dorling, Danny. 2019. *Inequality and the 1%*. London: Verso.

Dryzek, John S. 2000. *Deliberative Democracy and Beyond: Liberals, Critics, Contestations*. Oxford; New York: Oxford University Press.

Dusa, A. 2018. *QCA with R: A Comprehensive Resource*. London: Springer.

Esping-Andersen, G. 1990. *The Three Worlds of Welfare Capitalism*. Princeton, NJ: Princeton University Press.

Eurofound. 2012. *Working Conditions and Sustainable Work: An Analysis Using the Job Quality Framework*. Luxembourg: Publications Office of the European Union.

Exworthy, M., L. Berney, and M. Powell. 2002. '"How Great Expectations in Westminster May Be Dashed Locally": The Local Implementation of National Policy on Health Inequalities', *Policy and Politics* 30(1):79–96.

Foroohar, R. 2016. *Makers and Takers: The Rise of Finance and the Fall of American Business*. London: Crown Business.

Frank, Robert. 2007. *Falling Behind: How Rising Inequality Harms the Middle Class*. Princeton, NJ: University of California Press.

Frank, Thomas. 2016. *Listen, Liberal: Or What Ever Happened to the Party of the People?* London: Scribe UK.

Frankfurt, Harry. 2015. *On Inequality*. Princeton, NJ: Princeton University Press.

Freidson, E. 1988. *Profession of Medicine: A Study of the Sociology of Applied Knowledge*. Chicago, IL: University of Chicago Press.

Fukuyama, F. 2012. *The End of History and the Last Man*. London: Penguin.

Fuller, S. 2018. *Post-Truth: Knowledge as a Power Game*. London: Anthem Press.

Galbraith, J. K. 1958. *The Affluent Society*. London: Penguin.

Galbraith, J. K. 1975. *The New Industrial State*. London: Pelican.

Galbraith, J. K. 1993. *The Culture of Contentment*. London: Penguin.

Galbraith, J. K. 1996. *The Good Society: The Humane Agenda*. London: Sinclair-Stevenson.

Garthwaite, K. 2011. '"The Language of Shirkers and Scroungers?" Talking about Illness, Disability and Coalition Welfare Reform', *Disability and Society* 26(3):369–72.

Gawande, A. 2010. *The Checklist Manifesto: How to Get Things Right*. London: Profile Books.

Giddens, A. 1991a. *Modernity and Self-Identity*. Cambridge: Polity.

Giddens, A. 1991b. *The Consequences of Modernity*. Cambridge: Polity Press.

Giddens, A. 1994. *Beyond Left and Right: The Future of Radical Politics*. Cambridge: Polity Press.

Giddens, A. 1998. *The Third Way: The Renewal of Social Democracy*. Cambridge: Polity.

Giddens, Anthony. 2011. *The Politics of Climate Change*. Second edition, revised and updated. Cambridge and Malden, MA: Polity.

Glennerster, H. 1995. *British Social Policy since 1945*. Oxford: Blackwell.

Greener, I. 2005. 'Health Management as Strategic Behaviour: Managing Medics and Performance in the NHS', *Public Management Review* 7(1):95–110.

Greener, I. 2018. *Social Policy after the Financial Crisis*. Cheltenham, UK and Northampton, MA, USA: Edward Elgar Publishing.

Greener, Ian. 2021a. 'Comparing Country Risk and Response to COVID-19 in the First 6 Months across 25 Organisation for Economic Co-Operation and Development Countries Using Qualitative Comparative Analysis', *Journal of International and Comparative Social Policy* 1–15. doi: 10.1017/ics.2021.6.

Greener, Ian. 2021b. *Comparing Health Systems*. Bristol: Policy Press.

Hardman, Isabel. 2020. *The Natural Health Service: How Nature Can Mend Your Mind*. London: Atlantic Books.

Harris, Jose. 1998. *William Beveridge: A Biography*. Oxford: Oxford University Press.

Hay, C. 1998. 'Globalization, Welfare Retrenchment and "the Logic of No Alternative": Why Second-Best Won't Do', *Journal of Social Policy* 27(4):525–32.

Haynes, Philip. 2017. *Social Synthesis: Finding Dynamic Patterns in Complex Social Systems*. London: Routledge.

Hills, John. 2014. *Good Times, Bad Times: The Welfare Myth of Them and Us*. Bristol: Policy Press.

Hochschild, A. 2016. *Strangers In Their Own Land: Anger and Mourning on the American Right*. London: The New Press.

Hutton, W. 1996. *The State We're In*. London: Vintage.

Immergut, Ellen. 1992a. *Health Politics: Interests and Institutions in Western Europe*. New York, NY: Cambridge University Press.

Immergut, Ellen. 1992b. 'The Rules of the Game: The Logic of Health Policy-Making in France, Switzerland and Sweden', pp.57–89 in *Structuring Politics: Historical Institutionalism in Comparative Analysis*, edited by S. Steinmo, K. Thelen, and F. Longstreth. Cambridge: Cambridge University Press.

Ipsos MORI. 2012. *21st Century Welfare: Seventy Years since the Beveridge Report.* London: Ipsos MORI.

Jenkins, Stephen. 2015. *The Income Distribution in the UK: A Picture of Advantage and Disadvantage.* London: Centre for Analysis of Social Exclusion, LSE.

Jessop, B. 1992. 'Fordism and Post-Fordism: A Critical Reformulation', pp.42–62 in *Pathways to Industrialisation and Regional Development,* edited by M. Storper, and A. Scott. London: Routledge.

Jessop, B. 1999. 'The Changing Governance of Welfare: Recent Trends in Its Primary Functions, Scale and Modes of Coordination', *Social Policy and Administration* 33(4):348–59.

Jessop, B. 2002. *The Future of the Capitalist State.* Cambridge: Polity Press.

Kennelly, Brendan, Mike O'Callaghan, Diarmuid Coughlan, John Cullinan, Edel Doherty, Liam Glynn, Eoin Moloney, and Michelle Queally. 2020. 'The COVID-19 Pandemic in Ireland: An Overview of the Health Service and Economic Policy Response', *Health Policy and Technology* 9(4):419–29. doi: 10.1016/j.hlpt.2020.08.021.

Keynes, J. 1997. *The General Theory of Employment, Interest and Money.* New York, NY: Prometheus Books.

Kim, Myoung-Hee, Kyunghee Jung-Choi, Hee-Jin Jun, and Ichiro Kawachi. 2010. 'Socioeconomic Inequalities in Suicidal Ideation, Parasuicides, and Completed Suicides in South Korea', *Social Science & Medicine* 70(8):1254–61. doi: 10.1016/j.socscimed.2010.01.004.

King-Hill, Sophie, Ian Greener, and Martin Powell. 2021. 'Lesson-Drawing for the UK Government during the COVID-19 Pandemic: A Comparison of Official, Media and Academic Lenses', pp.49–66 in *Social Policy Review 33: Analysis and Debate in Social Policy,* edited by M. Pomati, A. Jolly, and J. Rees. Bristol: Policy Press.

Klein, Naomi. 2014. *This Changes Everything: Capitalism vs the Climate.* London: Penguin.

Krugman, P. 2009. *The Conscience of a Liberal.* London: Penguin.

Le Fanu, J. 1999. *The Rise and Fall of Modern Medicine.* London: Abacus.

Legrain, Philippe. 2004. *Open World: The Truth about Globalization.* Chicago: Ivan R. Dee.

Lijphart, Arend. 2012. *Patterns of Democracy: Government Forms and Performance in Thirty-Six Countries.* London: Yale University Press.

Lister, R. 2010. *Understanding Theories and Concepts in Social Policy.* Bristol: Policy Press.

Lund, Brian. 2017. *Understanding Housing Policy.* Third edition. Bristol Chicago: Policy Press.

Maleki, Ammar, and Frank Hendriks. 2016. 'Contestation and Participation: Operationalising and Mapping Democratic Models for 80 Electoral Democracies, 1990–2009', *Acta Politica* 51(2):237–72.

Marmot, Michael. 2012. *Status Syndrome: How Your Social Standing Directly Affects Your Health.* London: Bloomsbury.

Marmot, Michael. 2015. *The Health Gap: The Challenge of an Unequal World.* London: Bloomsbury.

Marmot, Michael, and Richard Wilkinson. 2005. *Social Determinants of Health.* Oxford: Oxford University Press.

Marshall, T. H. 1950. *Citizenship and Social Class.* Cambridge: Cambridge University Press.

Millar, Jane. 2009. 'Basic Income', pp.233–51 in *Understanding Social Security: Issues for Policy and Practice*, edited by J. Millar. Bristol: Policy Press.

Minford, P. 1991. *The Supply-Side Revolution in Britain*. Aldershot, UK and Brookfield, VT, USA: Edward Elgar Publishing.

Mooney, G. 2003. *Economics, Medicine and Healthcare*. London: FT Prentice Hall.

Mulgan, Geoff. 2015. *The Locust and the Bee: Predators and Creators in Capitalism's Future*. London: Princeton University Press.

Mullainathan, S., and E. Shafir. 2013. *Scarcity: Why Having So Little Means So Much*. London: Penguin.

Nussbaum, Martha. 2010. *Not for Profit: Why Democracy Needs the Humanities*. Woodstock: Princeton University Press.

OECD. 2014. *OECD Employment Outlook 2014*. Paris: OECD.

OECD. 2017a. *Denmark: Country Health Profile 2017*. Paris: OECD.

OECD. 2017b. *Health at a Glance 2017*. Paris: OECD.

OECD. 2017c. 'What Has Driven Life Expectancy Gains in Recent Decades? A Cross-Country Analysis of OECD Member States', pp.31–44 in *Health at a Glance*. Paris: Organization for Economic Co-operation and Development.

OECD. 2018. *How Does Australia Compare?* Paris: OECD.

Offer, A. 2006. *The Challenge of Affluence*. Oxford: Oxford University Press.

Oliver, M. 1996. 'Social Learning and Macroeconomic Policy in the UK since 1979', *Essays in Economic Business History* 14:117–31.

Painter, A., and C. Thoung. 2015. *Creative Citizen, Creative State: The Principled and Pragmatic Case for a Universal Basic Income*. London: RSA.

Pariser, Eli. 2012. *The Filter Bubble: What the Internet is Hiding from You*. London: Penguin.

Peters, B. Guy. 2019. *Institutional Theory in Political Science: The New Institutionalism*. 4th edn. Cheltenham, UK and Northampton, MA, USA: Edward Elgar Publishing.

Peterson, A., and D. Lupton. 1996. *The New Public Health: Health and Self in the Age of Risk*. London: Sage.

Picketty, Thomas. 2014. *Capital in the Twenty-First Century*. Cambridge, MA: Harvard University Press.

Putnam, R. 2001. *Bowling Alone: The Collapse and Revival of American Community*. New York, NY: Simon & Schuster.

Ragin, C. 2008. *Redesigning Social Inquiry: Fuzzy Sets and Beyond*. Chicago, IL: University of Chicago Press.

Ragin, C. 2014. *The Comparative Method: Moving Beyond Qualitative and Quantitative Strategies*. Oakland, CA: University of California Press.

Ragin, Charles. 2000. *Fuzzy-Set Social Science*. Chicago, IL: University of Chicago Press.

Reibling, Nadine, Mareike Ariaans, and Claus Wendt. 2019. 'Worlds of Healthcare: A Healthcare System Typology of OECD Countries', *Health Policy* 123(7):611–20. doi: 10.1016/j.healthpol.2019.05.001.

Reich, R. 2009. *Supercapitalism: The Battle for Democracy in an Age of Big Business*. London: Icon Books.

Runciman, David. 2018. *How Democracy Ends*. London: Profile Books.

Saunders, Peter. 2013. 'Beyond Beveridge: Restoring the Contributory Principle to Retirement Pensions and Welfare Benefits', London: Civitas.

Savage, M. 2021. 'Calls for a New Beveridge Report as Numbers of Destitute UK Households Doubles during COVID', *The Observer*, 20 February.

Schneider, C., and C. Wagemann. 2012. *Set-Theoretical Methods for the Social Sciences*. Cambridge: Cambridge University Press.

Schneider, E., D. Sarnak, D. Squires, A. Shah, and M. Doty. 2017. *Mirror Mirror 2017*. New York, NY: Commonwealth Fund.

Shipman, Tim. 2016. *All Out War: The Full Story of How Brexit Sank Britain's Political Class*. London: William Collins.

Smith, J., and K. Walsh. 2001. 'The "Redisorganisation" of the NHS', *British Medical Journal* 1262–63.

Standing, G. 2014. *The Precariat: The New Dangerous Class*. London: Bloomsbury.

Steinmo, S., and J. Watts. 1995. 'It's the Institutions, Stupid! Why Comprehensive National Health Insurance Always Fails in America', *Journal of Health Politics, Policy and Law* 20(2):329–72.

Stiglitz, Joseph. 2003. *Globalization and Its Discontents*. London: Penguin.

Stiglitz, Joseph, Amartya Sen, and Jean-Paul Fitoussi. 2010. *Mismeasuring Our Lives: Why GDP Doesn't Add Up*. London: New Press.

Taubes, G. 2008. *The Diet Delusion*. London: Vermillion.

Taylor-Gooby, P. 2013. *The Double Crisis of the Welfare State and What We Can Do About It*. Basingstoke: Palgrave Macmillan.

Thelen, K. 2014. *Varieties of Liberalization and the New Politics of Social Solidarity*. Cambridge: Cambridge University Press.

Timmins, N. 2017. *The Five Giants: A Biography of the Welfare State*. London: William Collins.

Van Reybrouck, David. 2016. *Against Elections: The Case for Democracy*. London: Vintage Digital.

Viebrock, Elke, and Jochen Clasen. 2009. 'Flexicurity and Welfare Reform: A Review', *Socio-Economic Review* 7(2):305–31.

Vis, B. 2007. 'States of Welfare or State of Workfare? Welfare State Restructuring in 16 Capitalist Democracies, 1985–2002', *Policy & Politics* 35(1):105–22.

Wendt, Claus. 2009. 'Mapping European Healthcare Systems: A Comparative Analysis of Financing, Service Provision and Access to Healthcare', *Journal of European Social Policy* 19(5):432–45. doi: 10.1177/0958928709344247.

Wilkinson, Richard, and Kate Pickett. 2010. *The Spirit Level: Why Equality Is Better for Everyone*. London: Penguin.

Williams, F. 1989. *Social Policy: A Critical Introduction*. Cambridge: Polity Press.

Wilsford, D. 1994. 'Path Dependency, or Why History Makes It Difficult, but Not Impossible, to Reform Health Care Services in a Big Way', *Journal of Public Policy* 14:251–83.

Winter, J. M. 1980. 'Military Fitness and Civilian Health in Britain during the First World War', *Journal of Contemporary History* 15(2):211–44.

World Health Organization. 2000. *The World Health Organisation Report 2000: Health Systems Improving Performance*. Geneva: World Health Organization.

# Index

Printed and bound by CPI Group (UK) Ltd, Croydon, CR0 4YY

09/06/2025

14685770-0005